I0024081

RETHINKING THE CITY

STEVEN LIAROS

ON THE BIRTH AND DEATH
OF ECONOMICS, RELIGION AND DEMOCRACY
AND HOW WE ARE COLLECTIVELY...

ЯETHINKING
THE CITY

POLISPLAN

A PolisPlan Publication
www.polisplan.com.au

First published in Australia in 2014 by
PolisPlan - Ecovillage planners, project managers and publishers
Sydney, Australia
www.polisplan.com.au

Copyright © Steven Liaros 2014

This book is copyright. Apart from any fair dealing for the purpose of private study, research, criticism or review, as permitted under the Copyright Act 1968, no part may be reproduced by any process without written permission. Inquiries should be addressed to the publisher.

National Library of Australia Cataloguing-in-Publication entry (pbk)
    Author: Liaros, Steven, author.
    Title: Rethinking the city / Steven Liaros.
    ISBN: 9780992517106 (paperback)
    Notes: Includes bibliographical references.
    Subjects: Urban ecology (Sociology)—Forecasting.
                        Cities and towns—Social aspects.
                        Technology and civilization.
                        Social prediction.
                        Social evolution.
                        Internet—Social aspects
                        Urbanization—Social aspects.
    Dewey Number: 307.76

Other available formats:
ISBN: 978-0-9925171-1-3 (ePub edition)
ISBN: 978-0-9925171-2-0 (Kindle edition)

Cover Design and formatting by Scarlett Rugers Design www.scarlettrugers.com
Editing and review by Laura Daniel www.laura-daniel.com
With thanks to Prof Paul Burton, Dr Bill Metcalf and A/Prof Wendy Steele –
Griffith University, School of Environment and Urban Research Program.

"A man is but the product of his thoughts.
What he thinks, he becomes."

~Mahatma Gandhi

"This City is what it is because our
citizens are what they are"

~Plato

Steven Liaros is a consulting town planner, who also holds a degree in Civil Engineering and a Masters in Environmental Law. He continues a life-long passion for exploring ideas that contribute to his understanding of how the world works and towards his search for the Truth. This has led to an exploration of collaborative ideas for sustainable cities. To complement his inner journey, Steven has also visited, and volunteered at, numerous diverse communities in Europe, India, Sri Lanka and Australia.

to

Nilmini De Silva,
who encouraged, challenged and supported me,
who helped me discover the outside world, and
who gifted me the time and space
in which to create this work

with thanks to family and friends for their support.
This was possible only because
friends held up a mirror and helped me to see myself,
Nillie, Marianne, Con, Rob, Yanni and
especially Katherine, who taught me how to live with courage

for
Peter, Rania, Penelope, Jana, Penelope, Marissa, Peter,
Constance, Lia, Atticus, Amelia, Annabel...
and all their generation

CONTENTS

SYMBOLS

HEBREW – STAR OF DAVID
GREEK – HEXAGRAM

INDIAN – ANAHATA
(Heart Chakra)

CHINESE – HEXAGRAM
(one example of 64 patterns
of yin and yang lines)

CHINESE – TAIJITU
(Taoist symbol for
yin-yang harmony)

1200 BCE

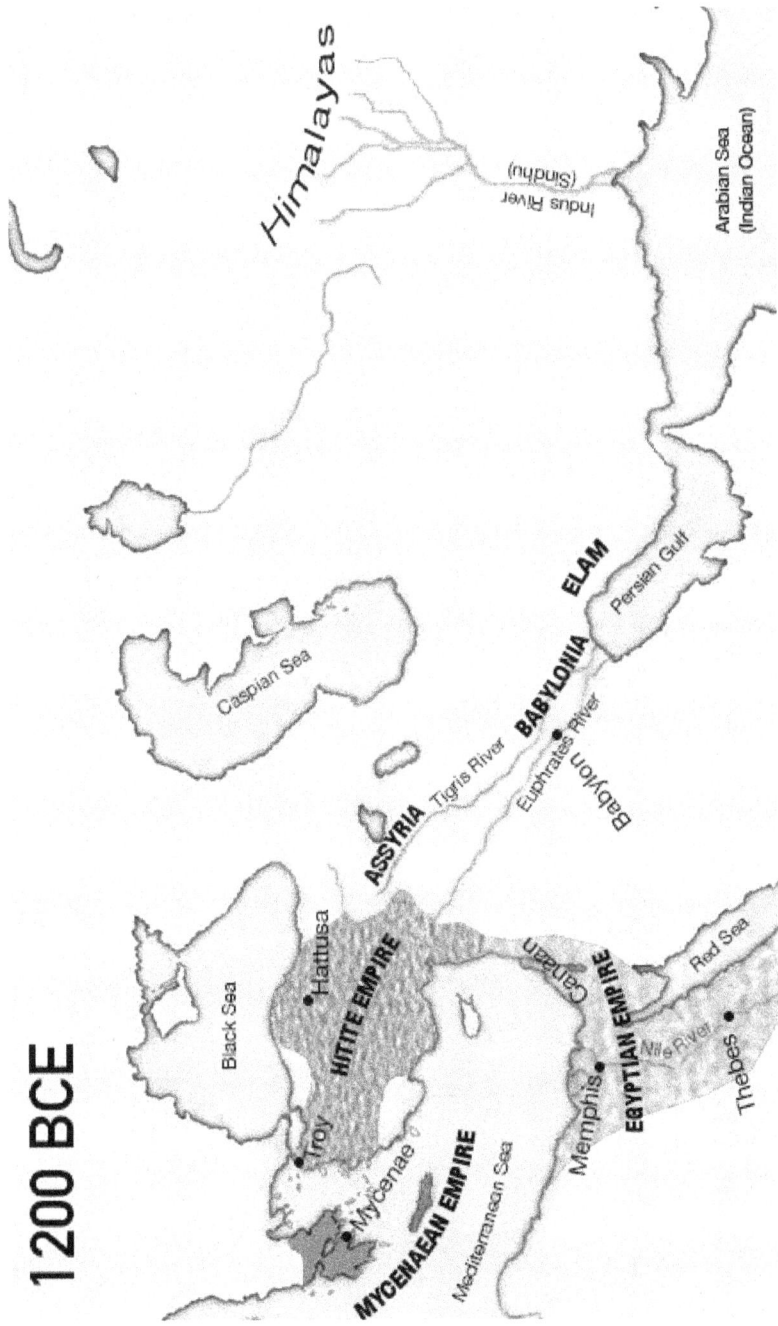

Himalayas

Arabian Sea
(Indian Ocean)

Indus River
(Sindhu)

ELAM

Persian Gulf

BABYLONIA

Caspian Sea

ASSYRIA

Tigris River

Euphrates River

Babylon

Black Sea

Hattusa

HITTITE EMPIRE

Troy

Mycenae

MYCENAEAN EMPIRE

Mediterranean Sea

Canaan

EGYPTIAN EMPIRE

Red Sea

Memphis

Nile River

Thebes

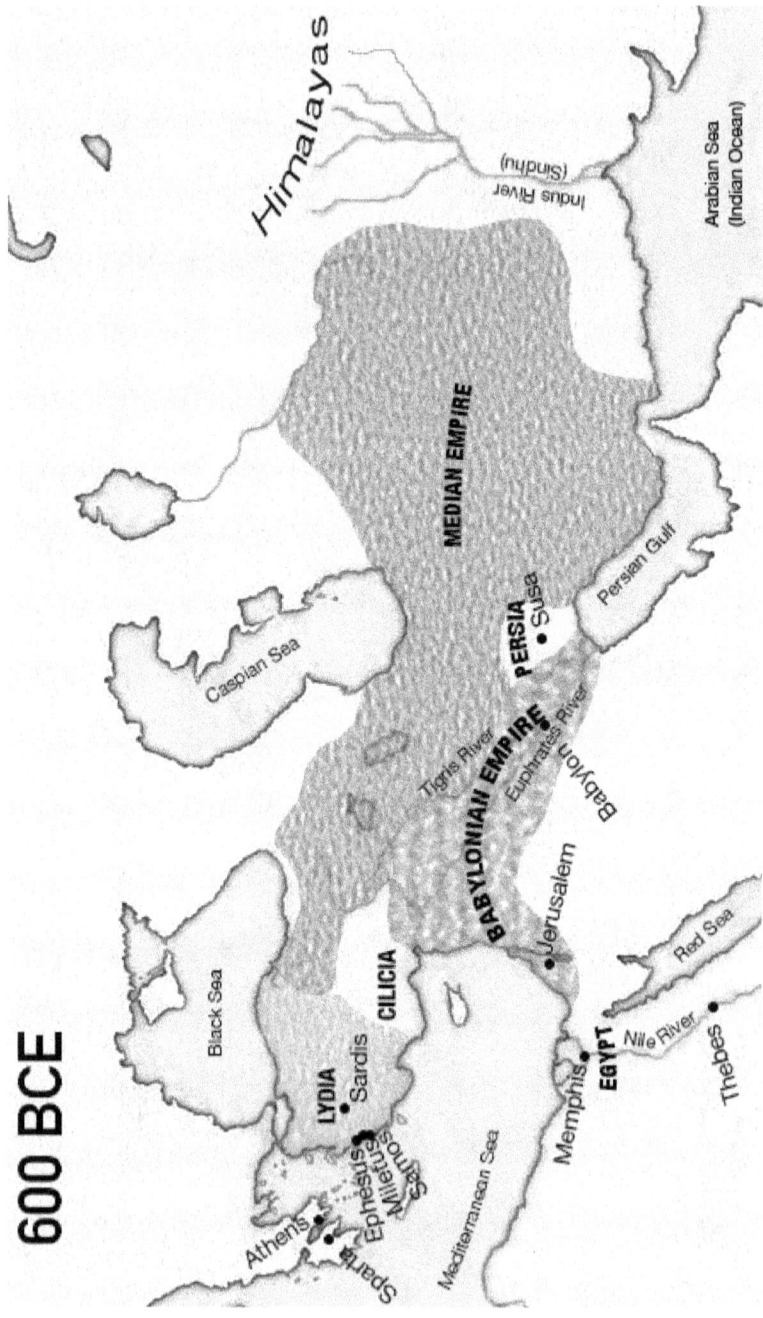

600 BCE

MEDIAN EMPIRE

BABYLONIAN EMPIRE

PERSIA
Susa

Babylon

Euphrates River

Tigris River

Jerusalem

Caspian Sea

Black Sea

LYDIA
Sardis

CILICIA

Samos
Ephesus
Miletus

Athens
Sparta

Mediterranean Sea

Memphis

EGYPT
Nile River

Thebes

Red Sea

Persian Gulf

Arabian Sea
(Indian Ocean)

Indus River
(Sindhu)

Himalayas

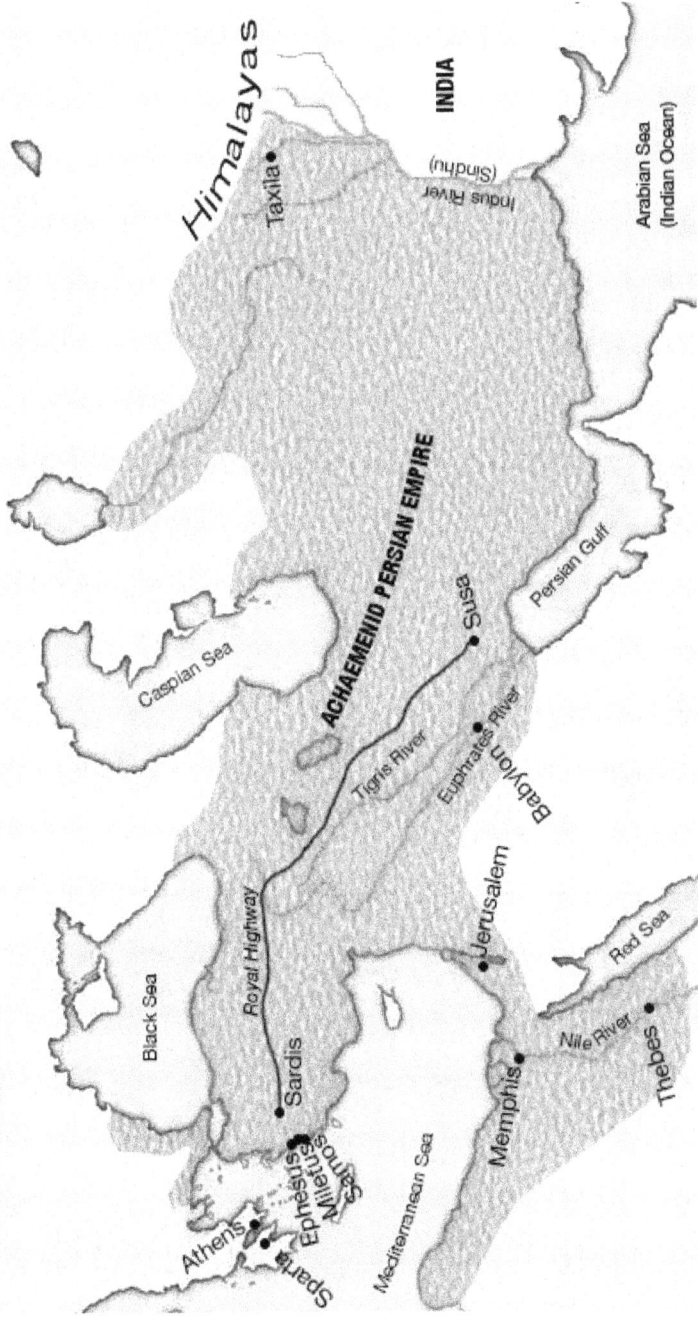

500 BCE

ACHAEMENID PERSIAN EMPIRE

Himalayas

INDIA

Taxila

Indus River (Sindhu)

Arabian Sea (Indian Ocean)

Caspian Sea

Persian Gulf

Susa

Tigris River

Euphrates River

Babylon

Royal Highway

Jerusalem

Black Sea

Sardis

Red Sea

Nile River

Memphis

Thebes

Ephesus
Miletus
Samos

Athens

Sparta

Mediterranean Sea

1
FATE OR DESTINY

Fate has been generous to me.

I was born to honest, loving, educated and generous parents who ensured that I was offered all possible opportunities in life, and their lives were examples I could follow. I had brothers to play and fight with, to respect and to trust, who would share my joys and on whom I would later rely when I felt most alone. I was also born in Australia, the lucky country, in the mid-1960s, so my early years were a period of national prosperity in which healthcare and education were free, the society was stable and orderly, and the world seemed carefree.

Fate was less generous to my father.

He was born during the Great Depression and lived his early years in a small fishing village on a scorched and relatively barren Greek island. Of course, the Depression, and global economics generally, will have less impact on a fishing village than on major cities. So long as there are fish in the sea, there will be work for the fishermen, food on the table and a commodity to trade for other necessities. Such a high dependency on one resource, though, meant that when the fishermen were called away to fight in WWII, the whole village went hungry. The Greek Civil War immediately followed and so the suffering for villagers continued. Despite excelling at school and studying law in Athens, my father looked around at a wrecked country and realised that there were very few opportunities at all, and none for an outsider who had no connections amongst the city elite.

Taking his destiny into his own hands he left Greece for a better life in Australia and arrived in the late 1950s in a country enjoying prosperity and stability. Together with free education, healthcare and other public services, the social stability guaranteed opportunities for *all* citizens. This meant that the hard work of the individual could lead to financial wealth or personal success, however defined. This was the unwritten social contract between the government and the citizens; in exchange for taxation the government would provide the basics, public infrastructure and services, as well as the stability in which the market could operate to provide other goods and services. The contract was that if you worked hard you could access more goods and services, but the basic public services were freely available to everyone.

This comparison of lives points to some of the central questions of this book. The first question is whether local communities are more resilient than large cities. Must we necessarily participate in the global economy in order to provide for our basic needs? Either way, there is more to life than satisfying necessities; what about more complex needs, exciting challenges and pursuits that involve others outside our local community? Can we imagine an alternative social model that perhaps operates like a decentralised network of local communities? A model that could allow us to challenge ourselves, to satisfy complex needs, share rarer skills and also to enjoy some of the more valuable benefits of the modern world, including its technology and the connectivity of the internet?

Other questions I will explore relate the ideas of 'government' and of 'representative democracy' asking whether 'representation' actually limits, or even precludes, civic participation. What is 'government' and where does it gain the authority to enter into a contract with real persons? We often speak of the responsibilities of citizens, but what might be the minimum responsibilities of a government to its citizens? That is, there should be benefits and obligations for both sides participating in a social contract. Is it possible for people to make social contracts, or collective agreements, directly with others within their community rather than through the medium of governments?

What are the most basic responsibilities of the collective to the individual? Is it education and healthcare? What about food and housing? Should fate determine who should be offered food and housing? Should fate decide who should have other opportunities? What are the responsibilities of the fortunate towards those to whom fate was less generous?

Another important theme relates to the consequences for a society of inequality. That is, if fate is generous to some in a society and not to others, how will the two groups regard one another, and will their worldviews differ? Perhaps those born into unpredictable circumstances might wish to hold on to the few things that offer certainty, permanence and stability. In contrast, if fate was generous to you and you were born into a stable, secure and carefree environment you may likely see the world very differently. Perhaps the fortunate will regard stability and certainty as a gilded cage and so will seek to explore, travel and strive for change. Could these differing perspectives create the change-seeking liberal and the stability-seeking conservative? Do these differing fates create the tension between liberals and conservatives that appears to be present in societies throughout the world, irrespective of culture?

These issues suggest that it is important to understand what fate is and how it relates to destiny.

§

The gods envy us. They envy us because we are mortal, because any moment may be our last. Everything is more beautiful because we're doomed.
                                        ~Achilles, from the movie *Troy*

This quote, from the movie version of the *Iliad*, captures in a few sentences Homer's most important theme. It is a theme that was likely one of the earliest triggers for much of the philosophical and religious questioning of the ancient world. Why, though, does Homer suggest that the gods envy us because we are mortal?

All the gods were allocated a task or responsibility at their birth, god of the sea, god of the hunt, messenger of the gods. This will remain their responsibility for all their infinite, immortal lives. Men on the other hand, *can* change the course of their lives. In this way, Homer sought to draw a distinction between fate, the responsibilities allocated to you, and destiny, your chosen deeds, or direction in life.

In this book I also argue that fate can still determine the course of our lives unless we *act* to change our lives for the better and pursue our destiny. Homer's expression of this idea resulted in the creation of many of the foundational ideas of our societies today. Is it inevitable that our lives are predetermined by fate? What power can we exercise over our own destiny? Let's examine these questions more thoroughly.

Imagine your 'destiny' as the one thing that you feel you must finish before you die—not something that it would be nice to do but something you feel compelled to do because it would show the world who you really are, it would distinguish you, give meaning to your life because through this one thing you would feel that you had contributed to making the world a better place. The doers of great deeds were the heroes described by Homer, whose glory and great names live eternally.

Unfortunately, if you are immortal, or don't acknowledge your mortality, there would be no incentive to finish your great deed! If you are not going to die, what's the rush? It is only the awareness of our mortality that drives us to pursue our destiny, to live more fully, to *change* ourselves for the better and, hopefully, through this to make the world a better place.

We could, then, define destiny as '*change* directed at perfecting yourself before you die'. So what about fate? The Greek word for fate, '*μοίρα*' (pronounced 'meera') is derived from a word that means 'allotted share'. So your fate is the share that was allotted to you at your birth, your lot in life.

Some were born in prosperous cities and others not; some were born rich, some poor; some were born aristocrats, others slaves; some male, others female; some dark skinned and others light skinned. These characteristics and their associated material gifts and 'place' in society, represent the share of the world allotted to you at your birth. They are your fate that potentially determines the course of your life.

Homer's question, then, is: Are you forever focussed on the circumstances of your birth, or are you reshaping, recreating and perfecting yourself? Are you shaping a destiny that frees you from your birth conditions? What determines your lot in life? Are you concerned more about what you were given or about the great deeds you can do before you die? Do you think that you are an immortal and that there is no rush?

I write about 'rethinking' the City in the sense that the City is what the citizens make it. Are we active in improving our City or do we passively accept what was given to us?

Before answering Homer's question, we might ask: Why is fate described as your allotted *share*, a share of what? If we think of a city-state in Ancient Greece, its territory was clearly defined and individuals belonged to their place. If they travelled they were known by the City they belonged to. Within the City, which was self-governing, independent and in full control of the resources in its territory, the citizens needed to find a way of determining who had what responsibilities. This can relate to, for example, the government of the city. In a democratic city, no single person has exclusive rights to govern, so there must be a way of determining who has what share. Similarly, no single person owns all the resources so again, there must be a way of determining who has what share. In this book, the word 'City' (with a capital 'C') shall be used to refer to the 'whole' City when considering the question of who has what share of it. So this book is essentially about the relationship between the City and the citizen. To what share of the 'whole' City should each citizen be entitled and what is each person's share of the 'whole' of the responsibilities?

In the example of the Greek city-state, the City is understandable as a discrete 'whole' because we are speaking of resources or goods or political power within a definable area that contains a discrete and identifiable group of people, but what about knowledge? In the case of knowledge the 'whole' would mean all the ideas and knowledge of the then Greek-speaking world, which is shared with many other cities. The question of fate and destiny can arise here also. Is fate more generous to some cities than to others? Does fate determine who has access to ideas and knowledge, that is, are the citizens of all cities equally entitled to equivalent opportunities for education?

Therefore, in some circumstances the 'whole' extends beyond the physical territories of a particular city. In our times, when we are governed on a national level and resources and economies are globalised, then thinking about our share of the 'whole' could mean that we need to think globally and ask: 'To what share of the planet is each person entitled?' We could also ask: 'To what share of the whole body of human knowledge is each individual entitled?'

In my view, this fluid nature of what is meant by the 'whole', and 'our share of the whole' reinforces the need to use the word City as the archetypal place in which we gather to determine who gets what share—of environmental resources, of the body of human knowledge and of political voice.

As for Homer's question regarding your fate and your destiny, hold on to your thoughts!

2

THE PUBLIC AND
THE PRIVATE

No man is an island entire of itself; every man is a piece of the continent, a part of the main. ... Any man's death diminishes me, because I am involved in mankind. And therefore never send to know for whom the bell tolls: it tolls for thee.

-John Donne

Before proceeding too far I would also like to explain why I believe it is critically important to rethink the way we build our cities with respect to the pressing issues of today.

I have so far defined the City as: *the 'whole' of which we are a part.* This approach can, I believe, be contrasted with the more familiar terminology that we use in relation to cities—that is, the 'public' and the 'private' domains. Our usual understanding of these terms is that they are clearly separated and distinct environments. We might say that we work in the private sector *or* in the public sector. We may refer to our residential property as 'my private domain' believing that the city's public land is on the other side of the fence. Yet we regularly cross over that boundary so as to be part of the City, and the City does have significant influence over our 'private' land and its uses. So it would, in fact, be more accurate to understand the 'private domain' as a part of the 'whole' or 'public' City.

If we use this approach and regard our private property as a part of the City rather than as separate from it, it becomes obvious that the more we collect for our own private and exclusive use, the less is available for others. It is not just individuals who do this but larger groups such as corporations. Therefore private interests should be understood as the interests of an individual or group that collects property, knowledge or political influence for itself to the exclusion of other parts of the 'whole' City.

To pursue the public interest is to pursue the interests of the 'whole', while to pursue private interests is to pursue the interests of a part of the 'whole'.

This usage of the words 'public' and 'private' should now highlight the urgent need for 'rethinking the City'. Debate about the relationship between the 'public' and 'private' has become all pervasive in recent years and covers numerous themes across a number of disciplines. For example, the Global Financial Crisis (GFC), has resulted in much debate about the respective roles and responsibilities of private banks and public authorities. Was the crisis caused by irresponsible banks or by ineffective government regulators? Are banks responsible only to their shareholders or also to the public at large—the 'whole' of the public? Should public taxes be used to bolster private banks? If taxes are used to support banks, do banks have a reciprocal obligation to support public authorities?

The collapse in property prices caused by the GFC has significantly impacted on the property development industry. Property developers regard themselves as the builders of our cities. Lower property prices reduce the viability of their current business model, resulting in significant political tensions. Developers argue that the development approval process, which is concerned with protecting the interests of the broader society and the environment, is simply an obstruction to development. Perhaps town planning can be 'improved', they argue, by reducing the need to consult with the local community? The tension between economic efficiency and the often complex and time-consuming process of engagement with other members of the community is the tension between private and public interests. Is the process of building a city to be an economically efficient one or a fully democratic one? It seems that both are not possible.

Private property developers also argue that requirements to contribute funds towards the delivery of public infrastructure also affects the economic viability of development. They argue that they have finite funds, yet the City also has finite funds. In this context the private-public tension asks: What share of the finite finances of a City should be allocated to the provision of public infrastructure so that all citizens have access to the basic necessities? Also, how and from whom does the City obtain these public finances? Whether it is development contributions or any other form of taxation, some private interests must be forfeited in order to increase the public purse. More deeply still, what are the City's objectives when taking money from private individuals for the public good? Is the money taken or is it given freely?

With the advent of the internet, other debates have arisen because, when we speak of information or documents that are 'in the public domain', we mean that they are freely available to, and accessible by, anyone. This has generated endless debate for lawyers concerned with intellectual property rights. Other issues also arise from the openness of the internet. Publishers everywhere are searching for new funding models because they don't want *all* information to be free. Many libraries are creating free online digital libraries; that is, they are putting more information into the public domain. There is an increasing demand for publicly funded research to be made freely available. Also, as evidenced by the WikiLeaks saga, nation-states are concerned about control over what information reaches the public domain.

The economic crisis and the internet are both fundamentally altering our perceptions of what is private and what is public, but any 'celebrity' will tell you that the media has never had any idea of what should reasonably be made public and what should remain private. The boundary between the two domains has always been a matter of individual interpretation.

Any discussion about the relationship between 'private' and 'public' is also mired in misconceptions, some of which arise because the meanings of these terms differ in different debates. For example, in classical economics, the market economy is the private domain and the government is the public domain. Yet in feminist literature, the market economy and politics represent the public domain, while the household is the private domain. In sociology, the discussion about private and public is about the relationship between privacy and intimacy against openness and sociability. With respect to information, the public domain is free, while the private domain is where knowledge and ideas can be bought and sold. How can we reconcile all of these perspectives?

I believe that the confusion stems, in large part, from the conception that the public and the private are separate. If instead we imagine the public as the 'whole' and the private as some portion of the whole, we can then ask questions such as: Why do some have a greater share than others? Is it always because they worked harder or smarter, or is it simply that fate was more generous to them?

With regard to knowledge and information: Should some people be entitled to exclude others from access to information and knowledge, most of which has been incrementally developed over tens of thousands of years by countless individuals working collaboratively with, or further developing the ideas of, countless others before, or should all the body of human knowledge be freely available to all human bodies?

With respect to the *market* and *government*: Are these separate and competing opposites, or could they be regarded as two complementary parts of the 'whole' City that would function better in cooperation rather than in competition? Are they already working in cooperation to the detriment of other parts of the City, the 'consumers' and the 'taxpayers'?

The feminist debate of the 1960s asked: Should women be locked into a part of the city, the household, simply because of an accident of birth? Similarly, should the vast majority of men be locked into the public domain, where they are bound by insurmountable debt, again simply because of an accident of birth? This brings us back to Homer's question: Should these accidents of birth determine the course of our lives?

Where did the current understanding of the relationship between private and public as separate domains originate? To look for origins we must, of course, examine our history and, in particular, the major events and ideas that have shaped the way in which we view our world. Why do we *not* naturally imagine our homes as a part of the 'whole' City? What caused the separation between private and public? What caused us to start building fences between us?

In the next chapter, 'Truth in History', I will begin an exploration of our earliest history so as to tease out the various elements of a City and their general origins. In Chapter 4, 'Adam's Dilemma', I will examine how the public and private domains came to be regarded as separate.

§

Throughout this book, I will be examining the origins of the foundational ideas of our cities: democracy, religion and economics—all invented ideas. All three of these ideas are currently mechanisms whereby individuals garner power and authority over others. My objective is to show how these ideas will be transformed when the underlying purpose is to ensure that all citizens regard each other as equals and so have equal access to the 'whole' City.

If the above ideas can be described as the foundations of our City it becomes possible to imagine the City as a physical construct built on the foundations of our *idea* of the City. It is our ideas that create the world we live in. If we re-imagine or rethink our ideas, we can re-create our City.

To illustrate this, cities are traditionally built around a central square, which offers an insight into the weight given to democracy, religion and economics in that place. For example, when the religious function dominates, the dominant feature might be the temple, church, mosque or synagogue. When the market dominates, the shopping centre becomes the centre of attention. The foundational ideas are those at the centre of attention in a City: Where do people focus their energies and efforts? So, in *Rethinking the City*, I will be examining these three functions and how they influence the character of a City.

As a practical example, in Islamic cities during the Ottoman period, the mosque was built simultaneously with a market bazaar and a range of public services such as a hospital and soup kitchen. This gave significant weight to the religious and economic functions but minimal opportunity for political participation. In contrast, during the early stages of the Roman Republic, significant weight was given to political participation but, as the republic transformed into an empire, such participation diminished, while economic and religious functions grew and the emperor was worshipped as a demigod.

3

TRUTH IN HISTORY

There is no god higher than Truth
~Mahatma Gandhi

A fascinating but little known fact is that many of the foundational ideas on which we build our cities were created within a very brief period in and around the sixth century BCE. At this time, Judaism was formalised into a religion, the Vedic tenets morphed into Hinduism, the founders of Confucianism, Buddhism and Jainism were born, Greek philosophy was re-invented and Athenian representative democracy was created. Just prior to these events the use of coins as a means of exchange began and, within the same century, the idea of money created the first global empire and the first international currency.

This period was followed by several centuries of intellectual debate until reasonably rigorous legal systems, such as Roman law, developed. No sooner had Roman law established its dominance, centralising control in Rome, than early Christian communities claimed that some things are not of this world, that some things extend beyond and above the law and the economy. Indeed they were arguing that decentralised local communities can more readily satisfy the physical and spiritual needs of their members than could a distant centralised authority. By the fourth century, though, Christianity had become an organised religion and was absorbed into the state structure with its associated economic system, creating the Byzantine Empire. Those communities outside the empire, particularly in the Arab world, argued that it makes no sense to institutionalise and centrally organise local communities. Eventually these communities would form the religion of Islam.

Sometimes the truth is in the detail, but sometimes a broader perspective sheds a different and unexpected light. In this book, I will employ the broad historical sweep because I am interested in the great ideas that have resonated with large sections of the human population. I am also interested in how these ideas developed over time, but only insofar as that development triggered another resonant idea. I am looking for the triggers and the resonance. What caused the people of the Indian subcontinent to come together under the Hindu banner? What triggered philosophical debate in Greece? What are the origins of Judaism and Buddhism? What were the social and economic circumstances that could have led to these? Who were the people who so influence our lives today? What can we learn from them, and can we reimagine our Cities? Most relevantly, what is this tension between centrally organised systems and loosely connected, decentralised networks?

Throughout history, the most enduring victories have been won not by the most powerful armies but by the most powerful ideas; and it is on these ideas that we build our cities.

I have chosen the title, *Rethinking the City* because, although the *subject* is cities, the *objective* is to provide a different perspective and to illustrate the power of ideas. To show how *thinking, rethinking, reimagining and perfecting* our ideas throughout history has changed the way we build our cities. If you love our cities as they are today, then its important to appreciate that they are this way *not* because people always conservatively accepted the way the world was but because some wanted to change the world for the better, they imagined a more perfect world. They did not accept fate, they pursued their destiny.

I would argue that the ideas identified at the beginning of this chapter, Judaism, Buddhism, Confucianism, Hinduism, coins as a means of trade, Greek philosophy and political representation, Roman law, Christianity and Islam, have each had a significant impact on the way we build our cities. I would also argue that they had this impact because they resonated with a large number of people. They resonated because people believed these ideas to be truths. So perhaps the truth can be defined as an idea that resonates with many people. The pursuit of the truth is therefore central to this project.

So what is Truth?

The problem with the question 'What is Truth?' is one of perspective. We may all find our own truth, which comes from our own personal perspective and experiences. The ideas we referred to above have resonated with *many* people but not with *all* people. We may believe, then, that these are truths for a part of the 'whole' only, truth with a lower case 't'.

Yet if we are able to set aside the above labels, especially of the religions, we will discover a number of commonalities—

Truths that cross cultural boundaries. So the aim is to uncover Truth with a capital 'T', a holistic or 'whole' truth.

Here I need to insert a note to say that although this book can only convey *my* truth, it also represents my pursuit of the 'whole' Truth. My approach is to pursue my truth honestly and then put it into the public domain where you, the reader, can judge whether it aligns with your own truth. So again, this book represents *my* truth and also *my* pursuit of the 'whole' Truth, which I will be able to confirm only if it resonates.

The pursuit of Truth requires objectivity because only from an objective viewpoint can you perceive the whole. This, in turn, requires that we approach the enquiry with an open mind. The consequence of this is that sometimes the Truth is not what you believed it to be at the beginning of the journey. For myself, being of Greek descent, I liked the common perception that many of the important elements of Western Civilisation had their origins in Ancient Greece. Some did, some did not. In one important instance—that Athens was birthplace of democracy—I discovered that what we call truth is, in fact, the opposite of Truth.

Objectivity also impacts on definitions. If we *define* Western Civilisation as the civilisation that started in Classical Greece, then we have simply *defined* this as the origin. Classical Greece, though, did not arise in a vacuum.

This objectivity with which Truth must be pursued requires that we constantly ask whether calling something the Truth benefits the 'whole' or any individual or group. It also requires that you follow wherever Truth leads you and that you not be constrained by the boundaries of our artificially constructed disciplines of knowledge such as religion (or any individual religion), history, philosophy, law, sociology, political theory and so on.

For myself, it was also not possible to pursue the truth according to logic and rational thinking exclusively. The scientific method, by which we grow the body of human knowledge incrementally, on the solid foundations of previous knowledge, is not sufficient. Such an approach suppresses our individual intuition and judgement. Reference books and papers that influenced or support my arguments are included in the bibliography at the end, but these simply represent aspects of my journey and potential further reading for you. I ask you to judge this book not on the basis of reason alone or intuition alone, but on whether your mind and heart align, whether the ideas are logically sound and also intuitively comfortable. Are the arguments internally consistent? Are they objective? Who would benefit and who would suffer if the ideas in this book represent the Truth or don't?

How can we distil the facts from the fiction to uncover this Truth?

§

Let's try to establish some Truths about the very earliest stages of human history through three of my favourite fictional novels, Jean Auel's *The Clan of the Cave Bear* and its sequels, *The Valley of the Horses* and *The Mammoth Hunters*.

The series is set about 25,000 years ago during the last Ice Age. It tells the story of Ayla, a young Cro-Magnon girl who loses her entire family as a result of an earthquake and then, after a period of aimless wandering, is adopted by a clan of Neanderthals. The Cro-Magnon were the earliest modern humans who, according to Auel, co-existed with the Neanderthals, another species of humans that would shortly become extinct.

The first book describes Ayla's development through childhood and into young adulthood as she struggles to fit in. She is taught the skills of the women by her adopted mother, who happens to be the clan's medicine woman. She therefore learns about all the various plants in her environment and their uses for both cooking and medicine. Secretly, she also learns the hunting skills of the men by watching them then practicing alone. At the end of the book, she is ostracised from the clan.

At the beginning of the second book, Ayla struggles to survive alone but soon enough finds a cave to live in, and her hunting and gathering skills guarantee her survival. She starts to enjoy some free time, but this has the effect of highlighting her loneliness. Her loneliness, together with her concern for an orphaned horse, results in the almost accidental 'domestication' of that horse. Some time later, similar circumstances result in the 'domestication' of a wolf. Both the horse and the wolf are regarded as friends rather than as possessions. They also greatly simplify hunting, making it, and life generally, more enjoyable and less lonely. While playing with some rocks by the nearby river, Ayla notices a spark fly and thus, by close observation of what happened, discovers the process of making fire by striking flint.

In a parallel story in this book, Jondalar and his brother Thonolan set out from Western Europe on a journey eastward.

They are young men, not yet twenty years of age, setting out to discover the world and themselves. They have no plan other than to travel as far as the journey takes them.

So where is the Truth? If you read only my summary and have not read the books, you may not know that I have omitted some of the most essential elements, the human relationships that are central to the power of these books. So it could be argued that I have not conveyed the whole truth. Yet I am not trying to convey the whole of *this* story but, rather, one aspect of the whole *human* story. This story describes the possible dating of some of the earliest stages of man's adaptation of the environment by domesticating animals—that is, the earliest steps of creating a City. Indeed, the first book describes how a clan of Neanderthals live cooperatively together, engage in joint efforts, benefit from each other's skills, and support each other. This illustrates how each member of the clan is a part of a 'whole'. They are a City in the sense that I have defined the term.

As for Ayla, her domestication of animals and her discovery of flint to light fires have the consequence of creating spare time or, freedom from work. This can result in a sense of loneliness but, alternatively, this spare time can be filled by building friendships or other relationships, or by play or creativity. I believe that this creation of spare time as a result of efficiently providing the basic necessities for survival is a universal Truth that would be a sound basis for building Cities. The use of that spare time for relaxation and enjoyment, as well as for creativity that can further improve the City, are also sound foundations for a City. The fact that these Truths are conveyed through a fictional story does not invalidate them.

Through Jondalar and Thonolan, we also recognise the value of travel. By seeing how others live, we gain a different perspective on our own lives. Travel also offers the opportunity to learn and share ideas. At this time, most people had learnt the skills essential for survival, so they didn't need to trade in food, they traded ideas, techniques and skills. They offered an extra pair of hands at the hunt in exchange for lodging, support and companionship.

In the third book, *The Mammoth Hunters*, Ayla and her new companion Jondalar (Thonolan had met an untimely end), join a clan of Cro-Magnon humans. This story is fascinating from the perspective of understanding how early societies may have functioned. It describes how misunderstandings can occur between people of different cultures and how these can escalate because people do not appreciate the perspectives of others.

The story also includes a scene that can only be described as democracy in action. A serious issue arises, so the chief calls *all* the clan members together and takes the position of chairman (my terminology). A ceremonial 'talking stick' identifies the person who is speaking and requires that the others listen and not interrupt. The speaking takes the form of a debate wherein anyone who wishes to speak can do so. The debate continues until *everyone* agrees on a course of action. There is no suggestion of a majority vote, as everyone would be impacted by the outcome. The close relationship with nearby clans meant that individuals could freely move between clans and so were not compelled to stay. If the clan valued the skills of the individual, they would also likely value that person's opinion because the person's skills and opinions come as a package.

The Mammoth Hunters also describes the housing of these early humans. Whereas the Neanderthals lived only in caves, the number of available and suitable caves thus limiting their numbers, these Cro-Magnon built their own shelters—large cave-like structures partitioned to provide separate sleeping quarters and some level of privacy. Here we see the earliest separation of private sanctuaries from communal spaces along with associated rules for entering into private spaces, such as closed doors prohibiting entry. Other design elements included a refrigerated basement for storing meat and other foods for the winter. During the Ice Age in these parts of Europe and Asia, the soil below a certain level was permanently frozen, even throughout summer, so the housing included a section that was excavated to this permafrost level for food storage.

The accommodation was also built near suitable drinking water and near the paths of migrating herds that could provide suitable meat. Here we can recognise the importance of the three most important factors that determine the value of property even today: location, location, location!

How much of this is Truth? I am not an archaeologist, anthropologist or sociologist, so I have not evaluated all the facts, or the arguments for and against this story, or the dating of these elements of our earliest societies. If they stored food surpluses, this debunks the idea that prior to the Agricultural Revolution people struggled for food and that it was only through agriculture that we started to generate food surpluses allowing us to stay in one place and build cities. It seems to me, though, that through the harsh period of the Ice Age, only the most adaptable and resilient would have survived. Such survival obviously depended on storing food for the winter period when there was little available and it was too cold to go out and hunt or gather.

I also have no specialist authority to verify whether societies operated on a democratic basis at this time. Intuitively, though, the story makes sense. If these early societies cooperated for the hunting and gathering of food and valued each other's contributions in these activities, they would more likely than not have valued all opinions related to more complex social issues. There is nothing overly sophisticated about democracy that a society with the capacity for speech couldn't develop. It simply requires that everyone has an opportunity to speak and be heard. It certainly makes more sense than the story that prior to the 'invention' of democracy in ancient Athens, societies invariably either fell into anarchy or were governed by powerful monarchs.

So, in terms of the human story and the story of Cities, I would argue that many of the essential elements of Cities were already in place from at least 25,000 years ago—far earlier than the Agricultural Revolution that is said to have commenced about 10,000 years ago and given rise to larger cities. That is, societies functioned democratically and all the citizens who were willing and able to participate did so. Societies had an economic system that included cooperation to provide for both their basic needs and trade between communities. Humans were already substantially altering their environment through the domestication of some animals, crafting of tools, and building accommodation, although alteration of the environment did not result in its degradation. They also had language in which ideas were stored and conveyed both between communities and through the generations. As a result of all of the above, individuals enjoyed plenty of spare time in which they could play, socialise and be creative.

This spare time can now be seen as the most important element in the ongoing development of cities. Spare time allows for the development of creative new ideas, which have the potential to create even more spare time.

As more and more ideas are shared across communities, technology for hunting and gathering food grows. Systems for housing are also developed, as are methods for storing foods. These ideas are stored in the language and are carried through the generations, each building on previous knowledge.

Essentially, cities are built on knowledge, and the development and improvement of cities depends on the open sharing of knowledge. Yet this only generates the question, which I will leave open: After 25,000 years of development, how much spare time do we have today?

§

Rethinking the City requires firstly that we understand what are the principal elements of a City. At the most basic level it is a system for providing for essential needs and, given that humans do this as a group, a system for managing group relationships— that is, an economic and political system. Both of these elements also depend on a system for sharing ideas, knowledge, skills, techniques and so on. They depend on communication.

To understand how the above systems have developed over time, we require a broad understanding of how our history has created the society we live in today. This is a principle known as backcasting. In contrast to forecasting, which projects current trends into the future, backcasting looks back to identify the origins of an idea. Some of the important cultural notions we live with today include the supposed difficulties of living 'in the wild' before the Agricultural Revolution, the tyranny of life before the advent of democracy, and the anarchy that would exist in the absence of laws and strong governments to enforce those laws. So where did these notions come from?

§

In *Ishmael*, Daniel Quinn uses backcasting when he asks: 'How did we come to be this way?' He looks back and identifies the Agricultural Revolution as an important turning point in human history because it changed the mindset of some humans. With the advent of agriculture, there were now two ways of looking at the world. The first way is that of the pastoralists, who saw themselves as a part of the natural environment around them. They lived off the fruits of the land. They hunted, but they also cooperated with 'domesticated' animals that at that time lived in a more collaborative relationship with humans—often within the same household. In these societies, human populations fluctuated according to the capacity of the natural environment to sustain them.

The second and newer way of looking at the world was the perspective of the agriculturalists. This group chose not to live off the spontaneous fruits of nature but to control nature. They tilled the soil in an identified area, planted seeds according to their perceived needs and then harvested produce. This required a lot more work, but there was no longer a strict dependence on the fruits of the earth. With early successes, the population of the agriculturalists increased, so more seeds were planted to support the increased population, only for the population to increase still further. This requires either greater efficiency in production or more land or both. We opt for both and the population increases again. Our spare time and creativity are directed at increased productivity. Our political systems are redesigned to obtain more land, usually through violence. As a result, the population has since grown inexorably, as have the demands on the environment. There is no way of stopping a system that has, at the most fundamental level, been deliberately unhooked from the rhythms of nature and designed to grow without any limiting or balancing mechanism.

Quinn's argument is compelling, and he reinforces it with the biblical story of Cain and Abel in Genesis. This, he tells us, is a story told by the Semitic peoples of the Middle East who lived immediately adjacent to the Fertile Crescent, the place where we believe agriculture originated. From Genesis (4:2):

> Now Abel kept flocks and Cain worked the soil. In the course of time Cain brought some of the fruits of the soil as an offering to the Lord. And Abel also brought an offering—fat portions from some of the firstborn of his flock. The Lord looked with favour on Abel and his offering, but on Cain and his offering he did not look with favour. So Cain was very angry and his face was downcast … while they were in the field, Cain attacked his brother Abel and killed him.

The story of Cain and Abel is the story of peoples who are neighbours and so should regard each other as brothers.

Cain represents the agriculturalists and Abel represents the pastoralists. In the story, God favours the offering of the pastoralists. Cain is obviously disappointed, but his response, killing Abel, would not change the way in which his offering was viewed. The killing is senseless and meaningless. Quinn suggests that the pastoralists would have watched in horror as their neighbours not only killed them for no apparent reason but also destroyed or transformed the natural environment on which all depended. With the advent of agriculture, the demand for land for that purpose would grow relentlessly, and so the land available for pastoral use is continually reduced—a process that was described through the metaphor of the ongoing persecution and suffering of the lamb.

From the pastoralist perspective, where life included plenty of spare time, all agriculturalists are cursed with never-ending work. Genesis 4:12:

> The Lord said … When you work the ground it will no longer yield its crops to you.

The earlier curse on Adam who was cast out of the Garden of Eden—that is, an environment where everything was plentiful—is even more graphic in illustrating the difference between the two lifestyles. Whereas the pastoralist lifestyle was tried and tested for thousands of years and provided plenty of spare time, the agriculturalist life was hard work. Genesis 3:17:

> Cursed is the ground because of you; through painful toil you will eat food from it all the days of your life.

Daniel Quinn's *Ishmael*, provides more detail about the consequences of the advent of agriculture. The crucial element, though, is not the agricultural process itself but the new way of looking at the world as something to be controlled and managed. Our focus therefore narrows from concern for the 'whole' earth to concern only for that small part of it that we are managing. This separates us from the natural world and we are no longer a part of it. We are concerned for the survival of a few species of grain and livestock and not all species. Our separation means that we also lose our understanding of the natural rhythms and cycles of the earth, which again separates us still further.

Our desire to manage the agricultural process and our continual failure to do so, only pushes us to try harder and harder to control every aspect of the natural environment, separating us still farther from it. We have seen how this results in perpetual demands for more land and more productivity, but it also justifies destroying anyone or anything that obstructs the satisfaction of those demands.

The more we make these justifications, the more we believe them. Those who are not part of the system are uncivilised and need to be taught the 'right' way of living. We have abandoned the Garden of Eden for the 'right' way—the way of hard toil and continual failure at an impossible project.

§

It is one thing to be separated from the natural environment but quite another to believe that that separation is the only and 'right' way to live. How did we come to believe this so fervently? How did we convince ourselves so well, especially since the pastoralists had so much freedom from work, while we agriculturalists are cursed with perpetual work?

4

ADAM'S DILEMMA

To Adam he said, "Because you listened to your wife and ate from the fruit of the tree about which I commanded you, 'You must not eat of it'. Cursed is the ground because of you; through painful toil you will eat food from it all the days of your life.

~Genesis 3:17

Imagine the dilemma facing Adam as the forbidden fruit is placed in his hands. God himself commands that he should abstain but his wife suggests that he eat it. There is more than a hint in this passage that Eve is using her feminine wiles and that Adam, like all men, willingly submits to ensure that he continues to be able to satisfy his most important private interests.

Some readers will now be thinking: how does everything end up being about sex, do all men think with their loins? Well, if we can reach the generalisation that all men seem to think with their loins, then perhaps this is a Truth. Perhaps rather than mocking and taking advantage of this natural trait, a conversation about Cities could include an acknowledgement of this Truth and a means of addressing it.

This parable is clearly not about tasting fruit, it is concerned with our choices, particularly the choices made by men, who perhaps should be more conscious of their decision-making processes, putting limitations on the extent to which these are motivated by private interests. What would be your honest response if questioned why you need to continually protect, enhance, increase and sometimes exaggerate your private assets? This is not to suggest that women are passive participants and they too could also be more conscious of this dilemma and their role in it.

The parable also encourages us to think about who holds the knowledge of good and evil and even if it is possible to hold such knowledge.

God, as described in these passages, is all-knowing, all-powerful and is everywhere and everything, so my interpretation of this would be that 'God' is the 'whole' of which we are all a part. So Adam's dilemma describes the tension between serving the whole City and serving his own interests, because one cannot serve two masters. Every moment, every action is a choice. Indeed, this story relates to a particular choice, one that is made daily in every household—the choice between 'spouse and family' on the one hand and 'finding my place in something bigger' on the other. It is the tension between the household and the City. It relates not only to the choices made by men but by women also and represents a central concern of the feminist debate. We *all* may ask, how do I enjoy a fulfilling home life as well as a satisfying career? Why do I have to choose and why can't I have it all?

To illustrate how this choice between the household and the City, translates into the way we build our cities, consider the substantial growth in suburban housing over recent decades. This represents the choice to provide more and more services within the household and rely less on the City, which results in bigger houses with less access to public infrastructure. Once the city is built this way, no amount of complaining to or about the government will make similarly expanded public transport feasible, so we become locked into the use of private vehicles and bigger households. This choice—to provide more and more within the household—also reflects the hope of eventually having it all, *owning* it all. Perhaps the issue for some is whether we actually acknowledge a dilemma here. Do all our choices and decisions favour the household, spouse and family?

The alternative choice is to live in smaller private dwellings in a more compact City with ample *access* to public facilities and services—as indeed, our earlier cities were formed. It is a simple, though perhaps not easy, shift in mindset from *ownership* to *access*. The recent trends towards micro-housing and co-housing may represent the beginnings of a shift in this direction.

Getting back to the historical context of Adam's dilemma we may ask: Why was this tension so vivid in the minds of the authors of Genesis? Who were the authors? In what context did they write? Apparently, the Genesis stories had a long oral history before being written down. These separate stories were in turn merged over a number of centuries and finally consolidated in their current form in about the 6th century

BCE, together with the other four books of the Torah. The Torah later also became the first five books of the Old Testament and formed the basis of both the Christian and Islamic faiths. Given the broad acceptance of these narratives, we must start by assuming that they describe certain Truths.

Traditionally, Moses is regarded as the author of the Torah, but he, his followers and successors told these stories orally for several centuries before they were written down. So do we know when Moses lived? There is some broad consensus that Moses or a Moses-like figure did exist and that his later years, when he would have led the Israelites out of Egypt, would have been in the early 12th century BCE.

What were the historical events or context of the life of Moses in which the story of Adam and Eve was first conveyed? The period from about 1206 BCE to about 1150 BCE is referred to as the Bronze Age Collapse. The Bronze Age empires of Mycenaean Greece, the Hittite Empire in modern-day Turkey and Syria and the New Kingdom of Egypt, which included the land of Canaan, all went from the peak of their power and into a spiralling decline. This was a multi-national cultural and economic collapse. The Greek Dark Ages are considered to have started in about 1100 BCE and a similar dark age, the Third Intermediate Period, occurred in Egypt from about 1070 BCE.

What is the relevance of the collapse of empires at the time in which Moses lived? Of course it must add credibility to the broad outline of the story of Exodus in which Egypt suffers numerous plagues, including sicknesses arising from unhealthy living conditions; poisoned water, people suffer from boils and the livestock also suffer pestilence. Other plagues— of frogs, locusts, lice—usually occur when the agriculture is not sufficiently diverse to manage the populations of different species. As a consequence of these plagues, the authority of the Pharaoh as a 'god' is diminished. The economy is also damaged through falling production, resulting in reduced income for the governing elite, while the costs of managing the empire, particularly food production, dramatically increase. Eventually, a large population departs or alternatively, the Egyptian zone of influence shrinks so that it no longer includes the land of Canaan or lands east of the Red Sea.

So these peoples who were formerly under the Egyptian yoke were now 'wandering the cultural and economic deserts'. They therefore needed to redefine themselves. Perhaps Moses had invoked earlier Semitic stories, such as that of Cain and Abel, encouraging his followers to return to a pastoral lifestyle. Indeed they would not likely have been wandering *aimlessly* in the deserts but would, rather, have actually defined themselves as wandering pastoralists:

> Then the Lord said to Moses: "I will rain down bread from heaven for you. The people are to go out each day and gather enough for that day… On the sixth day they are to [gather] twice as much as they gather on other days."
> ~ Exodus 16:4-5

If heaven is understood as the 'earth in perfection' then it is possible to appreciate that bread was not falling out of the sky but that the earth was providing the food needed for each day. It was not necessary to produce more, which would only attract locusts, and then store it in barns where it would become diseased. If we do not take more than we need, there will always be more than enough. Why then would Moses be advising to take twice as much on the sixth day?

Imagine for a moment entire populations whose lives, together with all their inherited memories, were those of servants or slaves in enormous empires—disenfranchised or disempowered peoples who were suddenly free. If such people were to redefine themselves, what would be the first principles of their new society?

In my view, former slaves would aim to guarantee freedom from work; at least some of the time. One would expect that a new society formed in this way would also be egalitarian; it would aim for equality for all. Everyone would share the work and everyone would have some free time.

> By the seventh day God had finished the **work** he had been doing; so on the seventh day he rested from all his **work**. Then God blessed the seventh day and made it holy, **because** on it he rested from all the **work** of creating that he had done. [emphases added]
>
> ~Genesis 2:2-3

The Sabbath is a holy day *because* it is a day of rest from work. Its purpose was to set aside the demands of work and the demand for greater productivity, so as to focus on family and community. The Sabbath and, later, the Christian Sunday were not intended to relieve us from the authority and demands of the economy only to submit to another authority. These holy days were defined as sacred *because* they provided rest from work, they provided *freedom* and the opportunity to engage and share with neighbours. We once left behind the demands of work and the economy for one day in seven so as to focus on personal and community development. Today, we no longer have holy days; we have a break, an escape or a vacation. We aim to separate or vacate ourselves from the daily grind, from the economy, but rarely with the conscious intention of finding a space for growth and development. We speak of recreation and do not appreciate that the word is *re*-creation, a time and place where we re-discover or re-invent ourselves through our interactions with others.

A key theme arising from the Exodus story is the demand for some freedom from work. Like an Egyptian Pharaoh, we claim today that ours is the greatest and most advanced civilisation in human history but, for most, it is just work, work, work! So a fundamental Truth that must be a founding principal of good cities of the future is that they must provide some freedom from work.

With respect to the impact of this on cities, we can see that for the first time we regard city life as formally divided into two parts: an economic part, where the work is done and the sacred part, which provides freedom from work. The Hebrew approach of dividing time, that is the days of the week, between work and freedom from work is dramatically different from the Greek approach.

Recall that the Bronze Age Collapse affected Greece as well as Egypt. Moses inspired the Hebrews, but other ideas surfaced in Greece. Just as the Hebrew traditions were conveyed only orally for many centuries, so were the Greek traditions that became Homer's epics. Homer is sometimes referred to as the teacher of Greece, as Moses is for the Hebrews, and their instructional stories, informed by the experiences of life under former empires, later became the foundational myths of their peoples.

Whereas Moses suggested a day of rest, the approach in Greece was somewhat different. Here the desire was not for rest from work but for the creation of a City in which the citizens were not trapped by fate but were able to pursue their destiny. Essentially, our common human fate is that we are natural animals that have natural needs such as food and housing, and these require work. There is no avoiding the fact that we must do some work to satisfy these needs. Yet how do we put limits on this work so that there is sufficient freedom to pursue our destiny?

The solution that the Greeks devised was to organise the City in a particular way that included the construction of the *symposium*, a forum for discussing matters other than work and the necessities of daily life. This allowed citizens to contain their work responsibilities and obligations within the private domain of the household, while the symposium and the public domain were places of freedom from work.

The symposium, like the Sabbath, represented a conscious separation of work, household chores and private interests from City life. Unlike the Sabbath, which separated the 'time' of the City, the symposium separated the 'spaces' of the City.

At the end of the last chapter I asked: How did we come to so fervently believe that the separation from the natural environment is the right way to live, even if it involves more work? If you think of work as something that is imposed on us by our natural needs, then to desire freedom from work is quite unnatural. Yet this desire for freedom seems also to be hard-wired within us. Spirituality is freedom from the limitations of the body. Creativity is freedom from the constraints of established ideas or ways of working. It appears that we have an inbuilt need to separate ourselves from nature.

Although I still maintain that a good City must be founded on the idea that the citizens must have some freedom from work, we must be aware that this freedom separates us from nature.

So the story of Cities again takes two divergent paths. The first divergence occurred with the onset of the Agricultural Revolution and the introduction of the idea of managing nature. The second divergence relates to providing freedom from work in two different ways. The Hebrew approach is to separate the 'time' of the City, while the Greek approach is to separate the 'spaces' of the City.

Our next step must be, therefore, to understand these two models more thoroughly. Chapter 5, 'The Star of David', describes the Hebrew model, while Chapter 6, 'The Theory of the Symposium', describes the Greek model.

5

THE STAR OF DAVID

To regard the Hebrew model for cities as one that simply aims for one day of rest in seven is to miss its most elegant elements. With the decline of Egyptian influence, Moses and his contemporaries were free to fully define a more beautiful society, and their objective would surely have been to learn as much as possible from the errors of the former empires.

Perhaps 'The Fall of Man' refers to the inevitable collapse of societies that are focussed only on the enhancement of private interests. Societies are destined to collapse if their citizens cannot see beyond their own self-interests or the interests of their gender, their family, their ethnicity, their nationality, their religion or other parameters that exclude others.

So the lesson of Adam's dilemma is that Adam should not always choose to pursue his own interests, not to *always* take the fruit offered by Eve, but should occasionally pursue the interests of the 'whole' City. This means that although, in order to sustain himself, he could pursue his own interests for six days in seven, he should, on the seventh day, sit amongst the community and share his wealth. This would have the effect of regularly recalibrating the community towards an equilibrium of equality.

In the Egyptian system, though, power was not enjoyed only by those who had material wealth. At the time of Moses, the High Priests of Amun enjoyed status almost equal with that of the Pharaoh. So Moses addressed the power of the priests also.

The god of the new society would have no name. If god can be named and understood, then some will always suggest that they *know* and understand 'him' better than others. Those who claim to know god more intimately, or to know what is good and what is evil are claiming to know what is best for others. This allows them to elevate themselves and impose laws. This elevation of those who 'know' god creates a hierarchy with the most 'knowledgeable' priests at the top and those outside the priestly class always being subservient.

Such hierarchies are not consistent with the desired egalitarian society and the striving towards equality. This is not to suggest that teacher-student or parent-child relationships are not hierarchical but that these relationships should be based on the assumption that the student or child is a future equal.

This idea was also embedded in the story of Adam's dilemma. The tree of knowledge of good and evil was forbidden not because of any objection to knowledge in general. In fact, Moses permits eating from any tree, essentially saying that we can 'know' everything *except* 'good and evil'. Today, our courts of law judge every case on its merits. Laws are assessed based on the circumstances of the action and the character of the actors. We appreciate that it is unjust to apply laws in an absolutist manner. The parable, in my view, suggests that no one can know 'evil' in such an absolute way, proclaiming particular thoughts and acts as sinful, as institutionalised religions tend to do. Perhaps it is time to acknowledge that there is no absolute good or absolute evil and that it therefore cannot be 'known'. Perhaps we should rethink the manner in which many secular, as well as cultural, laws are conveyed as lists of prohibitions.

The true god of an egalitarian society cannot be named because he is everyone and everything around you; he is the 'whole' City, including your neighbours and your environment. If you know your neighbour and your environment, you will love them as your god. Everyone will support and encourage everyone else. Conversely, if citizens need to enact laws to restrain each other, they are assuming that all citizens, including themselves, are inherently evil, that in the absence of laws, the society will fall into anarchy. To impose restrictive laws is to claim superior knowledge of good and evil over those to whom the laws are applied.

Both material wealth and suggestions of access to hidden knowledge are used to create divisions and hierarchies in our society, providing freedom for some at the expense of others. Systems for protecting private assets and private knowledge therefore support and maintain these divisions. An egalitarian society would support access to both wealth and knowledge for all, rather than ownership by a few.

To create this egalitarian society requires that everyone offer some of their work and time for the public interest, while also aiming to ensure that their private interests are satisfied. The dilemma for each of us is to find the right balance for ourselves. This will be different for everyone because everyone is different. Often social equality is interpreted to mean that everyone should give the same number of hours of voluntary work. I would argue that the creation of a society of equals starts with an acknowledgement that we are all different, that we all have different needs and that we all have different things to offer. A society of equals is one in which everyone *regards* everyone else as their equal despite these differences. It is a society in which everyone aims constantly to reduce material inequality and shares knowledge transparently. A public forum provides every single person equal rights not just to speak but to be heard. It guarantees every citizen freedom from work *some of the time*. The purpose of the public domain is to ensure that everyone feels that all their private needs are satisfied, including housing and other basic necessities.

There are only two options for a society: freedom for everyone or power for a few. Either the work is shared and everyone is free or the majority are trapped by work, responsibilities and demands for greater loyalty. In this second option, obedience to external authority takes precedence over community and neighbours.

These ideas were beautifully and simply expressed through a symbol that became known as the Star of David.

The Star of David is also known as the Hexagram, which in Greek literally means six marks, letters, notes, writings or epistles. Despite this Greek expression, the idea of six marks as a means of determining the 'divine will' more likely originates in China.

The Star of David is six marks forming two intersecting triangles. The ideas expressed through this symbol are amongst the most profound and universal ideas in human history. This symbol is found across the Eurasian continents including in Arabic architecture and many Eastern Orthodox Christian churches. In the Hindu and Buddhist traditions, the Hexagram is located in the centre of the heart chakra, or *anahata,* and is associated with freedom, emotional empowerment and hope. While the three lower chakras relate to instinct and bodily functions and the three upper chakras relate to intellect, consciousness and spirituality, the heart chakra is where the physical and ethereal are in equilibrium.

Two equal-sided triangles of equal size, overlaid one on the other, represent the perfect union of masculine and feminine. The upward pointing triangle, the masculine blade, points to heaven. The downward pointing triangle, the feminine vessel, points to the earth.

The opposing directions illustrate that although the triangles are equal, they are not the same and that, indeed, masculine and feminine desires pull in opposing directions. This distinction between equality and sameness is the first lesson of the Hexagram: that in striving towards equality we must acknowledge our differences—not only between the sexes but between all individuals. The acknowledgement of our differences allows us to 'see' and to complement each other so that the collective becomes greater than the sum of the individuals. By appreciating our strengths and weaknesses, we not only better understand ourselves but we then also know what we have to offer and when to ask for assistance. By contrast, when striving to be the same, we hide our flaws and weaknesses so as to 'fit in'.

The overlaying of the blade and vessel to form a star illustrates that these opposing desires must also be located in the same physical space and not in separate places, as in the Greek solution. The spatial separation of the public and private interests in the Greek approach creates Adam's dilemma, requiring him to choose where to allocate his time. When the choice is forced, private interests will prevail, resulting in a curse on all. Locating competing interests in the same place allows these to be confronted and resolved rather than separated to create future tensions and conflicts. It is therefore absolutely necessary to create a time and place for this to occur.

The competing desires are referred to as masculine and feminine, not male and female. They are intended to *describe* general inclinations rather than to *define* the nature of each gender in all cases. The union of the masculine and feminine represents the union of the heaven-seeker (or risk-taker) and the earth-bound (safety-first) home-maker. Both characteristics are present to different degrees in both men and women and also change in emphasis during the different stages of our lives. Our earth-bound characteristics refer to our physical or bodily needs, our three 'lower chakras'. The heaven-seeker within us is our desire for something better, something more perfect or more beautiful. The 'heaven-seeker' is different from ideas that attempt to define heaven as the home of the creator god, as the place of perfection and as our destination after death. These definitions define god so as to impose rules of behaviour by defining good and evil. Such rules limit freedom and creativity and preclude the opportunity to create an egalitarian society.

This desire for a more beautiful world, the search for heaven, is expressed through spirituality and creativity. It also drives our quests of discovery and our explorations for new places and new knowledge. This perpetual questing creates change both within us and, consequently, in the world that we build. The Star of David thus also describes the fact that change is inevitable.

Earlier, I indicated that the idea of the hexagram or six marks originated in China. The *I Ching* or *Book of Changes* is the nearly 5,000-year-old foundational text of Chinese culture and philosophy, and it also uses hexagrams but in a different form, composed of six stacked horizontal marks or lines. Each line is either broken or unbroken. The broken or open line is feminine, or yin, in character, while the unbroken line is masculine, or yang, in character. The *I Ching* uses the 64 combinations of broken and unbroken lines as a means of interpreting divine will. In conjunction with these hexagrams, numbered from 1 to 64, Chinese philosophy also adopts the flowing circular, black and white form of the yin-yang symbol, the *taijitu*, which represents zero and the perfect union of the masculine and the feminine. The masculine and feminine are two parts of the whole, the one flowing into, or transforming into, the other. This continual flow illustrates that we are perpetually changing and that the harmony between the masculine and feminine is possible only through the acceptance of change.

This concept of perpetual change, hidden within the meaning of the hexagram but beautifully depicted in the yin-yang symbol, *embraces* the two opposing human characteristics, the risk-taker and the home-maker.

In stark contrast, our modern societies appear to prefer competition and tension between these opposing desires and we are perpetually faced with Adam's dilemma—between women and men, between the home-maker and the risk-taker, between the private and the public, between the secular and the sacred, between conservatives and liberals, between science and religion and so on. As a result, we tend to choose our private interests and prefer security to freedom, productivity over creativity, tradition rather than a leap of faith, and our comfort zone more than a world of possibilities.

The heaven-seeker is the one willing to risk the safe and the stable for something greater, more beautiful or more perfect. The heaven-seeker is the one who pursues his or her destiny.

So the Star of David illustrates a society that seeks to *balance* the desires of the heaven-seeker within us, with the necessity to provide for our basic needs. In contrast, the Greek story told by Homer placed such a high value on the pursuit of destiny that the social system was destined to fall out of balance.

6

THE THEORY OF THE SYMPOSIUM

At the beginning of this book, I described how Homer encouraged the Greeks to pursue destiny rather than to be trapped by fate. Yet even when citizens are pursuing their destiny they still cannot avoid dealing with our common human fate—to do the work necessary for the provision of basic natural needs. The dilemma remains: Who will do this work, and how do you then create the opportunity for individuals to pursue their destiny?

The first part of the answer is to discourage the *sole* pursuit of private interests.

The Hebrews discouraged Adam from pursuing his private interests only through the curse of endless toil that would result from such pursuits. The Greeks created a derogatory word for those who focus exclusively on their self-interest. The Greek word '*ἰδιώτης*' (transliterated '*idiotis*') or 'idiot', simply means one who is concerned only for his private interests.

Unfortunately, whereas the Hebrew model sought to find a *balance* between private and public interests, the Greek model discouraged the idiots and encouraged the pursuit of destiny. We will see later that the Greek model did, in fact, seek balance, moderation and harmony, but the greater emphasis appears to have been on the doing of great deeds.

In order for great deeds to have value, they must be visible to other members of the public. This, in turn, required a physical place for the deeds to be done or displayed. The Greeks therefore organised the City in a particular way that included the *household*, or private domain, where work was done, the *symposium*, where ideas were discussed in a semi-public, semi-private forum and the public or *political* domain where the actions of citizens were visible to all.

This allowed citizens to contain their responsibilities and obligations within the private domain of the household, while the symposium and the public domain were places of freedom from work.

§

Dionysos, the Greek god of wine and theatre, could also be described as the god of the public domain. The wine that was drunk in the Greek symposium played a central role in creating a cultural idea that deliberately separated the household from the public domain.

The word 'symposium' is a compound Greek word, from '*sym* ' which means 'together' and '*posis*', which means 'drinking'. So a symposium was a forum where people drank wine together. It was a place where citizens interacted, debated, partied—a place of communion. The symposium was central to the Archaic (Pre-Classical) Greek understanding of 'city', of 'household', of 'economics' and of the distinction between the 'public domain' and the 'private domain'. The symposium was held in a room that was a part of the home but usually connected to the public square. It provided both a bridge and a clear separation between the public domain of the city, or the *polis*, and the private domain of the household.

The role of the host was crucial to the symposium because he was responsible, before the guests arrived, for diluting the wine. To the Greeks, diluting wine showed that, as a 'civilised' society, they were able to control, or manage, the use of alcohol. Their cultural system provided that when the host added water to the wine, it was an indicator that he wanted a serious conversation, and so the symposium would be a 'public' event. When he chose not to add water, the symposium would be a 'social' event where he was happy for his guests to get drunk. So the Greeks had a clear and practical way of distinguishing the 'social' from the 'public'.

The concept of a 'social' event is easily understood. For our purposes I'll call it a party or relaxed gathering; but to fully understand what they meant by 'public', it is important to appreciate why Greeks offered diluted wine and didn't instead offer, say, orange juice.

For the Greeks, wine was symbolic. The Greek god Dionysos was the god of wine, theatre and also of resurrection after death. You might ask what do these things have in common? Well, when you drank wine, you became different; you were no longer your usual or natural self. An actor at the theatre pretended to be someone other than his usual self and, of course, the resurrected self was not the natural self. The Greeks used the word 'ecstasy'—literally from 'ek-', meaning outside and 'stasis', meaning 'state', your physical or natural state—and so Dionysos was the god of ecstasy. When you were 'ecstatic' you were outside or beyond your natural state and this was important to their idea of the public domain. To enter the public domain, you had to drink wine in the symposium—specifically diluted wine—so that you could step outside your usual state. The Greeks believed that you had to step outside the private domain to enter the public. They were mutually exclusive. In the Greek mind, they were separate. The private domain was governed by necessity and the responsibility to provide food, clothing and housing. To enter the public domain, you had to first conquer the private domain. To be a free citizen, you had to be *free of necessity.*

This is reinforced by the word Greeks used for managing the household. The 'οίκος' (pronounced 'ekos'), from which we derive the prefix 'eco-', means household and 'οικονομία' (pronounced 'economia'), meaning 'economy', was the management of the household. The Greeks believed that the economy is the burden of our existence in the natural world. A responsible citizen would satisfy his economic obligations before participating in public affairs, which could then do voluntarily and as a free citizen. This domain of freedom was also where he could pursue his destiny and distinguish himself. Citizens would strive to complete their responsibilities as efficiently as possible so they could attend public events together with other free citizens. Freedom was freedom from economy, freedom from work, freedom from private responsibility. Only citizens who were free of economic responsibilities could offer the city a just government. The ecstasy of the free citizen standing in the public domain was an early expression of our idea of man conquering nature; but he conquered nature with the aim of being free to distinguish himself and to debate with his fellow citizens about how to build a good city.

This clear and deliberate separation of public and private domains through the use of drugs is not unique to Classical Greece. In the Americas, tobacco, hemp, chocolate and coffee were variously used, served the same purpose as wine in Athens, and were venerated in the same way. I sometimes wonder to what extent our drug addictions relate to our addiction to, or desire for, freedom?

When these ideas were rediscovered during the Renaissance, the separation of the public realm from the private was expressed through clothing. People wore fine quality, clean, colourful, elaborate and impractical clothing to differentiate themselves from labourers, to show that they were free. Hence the Italian love for fine clothes and your mother's insistence that you wear your Sunday best to church where you received diluted wine so as to commune with the divine.

The Renaissance, or Rebirth, relates to the rediscovery of the Greek ideas that had been retained in the East. Islamic households, especially in Turkey during the Ottoman period, were divided into the *haremlik*, meaning 'forbidden place' and the *selamlik*, meaning the greeting place. The forbidden place was a sanctuary and was reserved for women, while the greeting place was the public space for men.

Today, we white-collar workers have adopted the Renaissance idea of distinguishing ourselves from labourers through the clothing that we wear. We claim to show that we are free by ironing our shirts and wearing a *tie*. I like to call this the irony of the iron or sometimes the tyranny of the tie. We also purchase expensive material goods to show that we have the financial freedom to do so but, ironically, we fund these purchases by increasing our debt, a burden that limits our freedom. As our household, corporate and public debts rise, we are apparently showing each other that we are free. The need to show that we are free has become the burden that steals our freedom.

So this distinction between private and public, between work and freedom from work is, despite its corruption in practice, a foundational *idea* on which we build our cities. The private domain is the domain that focuses on private interests, on the economy, on self-interest, and this should not be overlooked. We need to provide for our personal necessities. The public sphere, on the other hand, is the place for focussing on public interests, on the interests of others who are not necessarily connected to us. It is the domain of selflessness, the place where we come together with our neighbours to deal with our common interests and to create a common culture; it is the place of compromise, where we forfeit a little of our own interests so as to build common assets and a common understanding of our collective selves—the place where we willingly *and freely* help others, where everyone benefits through the free contributions of others. It is not possible to be selfish and selfless at the same time. You cannot serve two masters. You must choose to be selfless. You must choose to create a public domain.

Earlier, I deliberately used the expression 'man conquering nature' because the Athenians were so enamoured by the idea of the public domain that, in their minds, it was justifiable to use any means necessary to conquer the private domain. This allowed them to justify slavery and the oppression of women in the household. Tyranny was justified in the household because it allowed the head of the household to become a free citizen. But, of course, the maxim always holds that 'the ends never justify the means'. It is not possible to cultivate tyranny in the household and expect that the free citizen will enter the public domain as a just man. It is not just about putting boundaries on economics but also about how you establish those boundaries.

According to the philosopher Hannah Arendt, "Man cannot be free if he does not know that he is subject to necessity, because his freedom is always won in his never wholly successful attempts to liberate himself from necessity." I would argue that revolutions invariably begin because one segment of society is doing all the labour while another segment has all the power. The Athenians justified slavery because their rhetoric suggested that somehow slaves would benefit by living in the greatest city or the biggest or most powerful city; but a great city is different from a good city. The Sabbath allows *everyone* to be free once a week. We need to create a time and a space in our cities that allows all people to be free—not bound by another set of oppressive rules, as required by organised religion, but *free*. We need to build a free public domain, and this should be one of the principal aims of Cities. How do we build homes, villages and Cities that assist us and free us rather than being burdensome, in terms of both maintenance and of mortgage debt?

Surely a more beautiful society would be one wherein the citizens freed themselves not by conquering nature but by mastering our understanding of it and of our part in it. Rather than separating ourselves from the whole, we could contribute to the enhancement of the whole for *all* its members (not just the humans). We would then be stewards of nature, working in harmony with nature to satisfy the needs of all.

In recent years, there appears to have been a significant increase in the number of attempts to build homes and villages according to the idea of reconnecting with nature. Eco-villages of all types are being designed and built with varying degrees of success. Many are guided by permaculture principles. Most are growing food, or at least their fruit and vegetables, on site. Solar power is the most common on-site energy provider. Buildings are being designed using passive design principles so as to minimise energy demand. The more adventurous are managing their entire water cycle, harvesting and purifying rainwater or a local stream for drinking, washing and irrigation as well as managing sewage and wastewater.

In my experience, most eco-villages also consider that the cooperation required to manage the environment and provide food, water and energy on site builds community bonds and therefore addresses social as well as environmental problems.

The arguments in this chapter, though, relate to the objective of providing freedom, or simply some free time, for the individuals living in that village. The idea is that by working in harmony with nature, more freedom should be available, yet most eco-villages I have visited are actually generating more work for the members of the community, while others add so-called 'environmental measures' that increase the total cost of housing and maintenance.

Perhaps it is too simplistic to suggest that the social, political and environmental problems we face today can be resolved by simply saying that we need to reconnect with nature or that we need to abandon modern fossil-fuel technology. Although reconnecting with nature is something we definitively need to do, I believe we firstly need to understand what this means. It is also equally important to create a cultural model that provides freedom from endless work because we will not be able to fully reconnect with nature unless we are able to create such a freedom-generating cultural model.

§

So how did the Greek model on which our Western system is based, and which so specifically strives for freedom, trap us into so much work?

The two domains we have described must, of necessity, be governed by two different sets of rules. I say 'of necessity' because the two spaces have opposing objectives. The rules governing the household relate to natural laws and the provision of food and other necessities. They also relate to contractual agreements that share the workload. By contrast, work or binding contracts are not consistent with the concept of freedom in the public domain. Given that the public domain was created as a space for freedom it must, by definition, preclude any requirement for work or to be bound by contractual obligations.

These new spaces—the symposium and the public domain—had no formal fixed rules. At each symposium, the participants were free to make up the rules to suit those participating. Having conquered their natural and essential needs, citizens invented other activities such as sports where they could start as equals and compete to see who would distinguish themselves. They also created theatre and art as ways of commenting on the public activities of others and on the economy from an objective viewpoint.

Creativity and excellence were born out of freedom from work and reflect a capacity for honesty and objectivity. Greeks believed that this was the very definition of a civilised society—one that made a conscious decision to create a cultural domain by placing limits on the economy and on private interests.

The problem with this 'solution', though, was that rather than offering freedom for everyone, the approach was to offer freedom to one section of the population. Women were not considered citizens, and the symposium was held in a room called the *andron,* the 'men's room' or 'men's place'—perhaps because the household was perceived as the woman's place, a space that was governed by women's rules.

This, of course, created separation and conflict between men and women. It also implied that all women always and only wanted to 'nest', to manage the household, and that all men always wanted to be free to explore, travel and seek the unknown. The response of the women was obvious, and the men were offered a choice. They had to choose between their freedom in the public domain and their wives, that is, their private interests. Eve offered the forbidden fruit and Adam had a dilemma.

Yet the game was not over. The rules of the public domain, which are always flexible, were amended to allow the participation of 'public women', creating a new tension between 'public' and 'private' women. As the rules changed further and more people were allowed into the public domain, there were too few doing the work. It was then 'justifiable' to take the citizens of other cities as slaves or servants with no public rights. Society thus became entangled in a perpetual competition based simply on who was entitled to be in the free public domain and who had to do the work.

The purpose of the public domain as a place of culture, art and creativity, a place for objectivity and honesty that allowed for the development of a cohesive and egalitarian society, was lost and forgotten. No longer were the citizens building assets that could be shared by everyone; instead everyone gathered more slaves to increase their own personal assets so as to show that they were more worthy than others to be free of work. Citizens were concerned only about jockeying with each other to decide who would be free and who would do the work. The public domain became a forum for the competing private interests of various groups in the society.

The consequence of this jostling is that you have to continually show that you are more worthy than others. This 'worth' is primarily measured on the basis of material assets, and so new ways must regularly be discovered for locking others into doing your work so as to enhance your material worth. This is the path of economic growth. It results in a small percentage benefitting from the receipt of taxes, rent and debt repayments, giving them freedom from work, while large sections of the population are locked into the payment of taxation, rent or interest on debt, denying them personal freedom.

In the absence of a designated time for all members of the community to come together and consciously recalibrate towards equality, there would be no way of limiting the race to grow private interests, which demands more and more work and ultimately results in slavery for all.

§

As these two models—the Hebrew and the Greek forms of Cities—were evolving in the manner we have described, a new development changed everything. In the land of Lydia, which is in modern-day Turkey and so immediately between the Greek and Hebrew worlds, coins were developed as a means of exchange.

From about 600 BCE it was no longer necessary to negotiate with neighbours, to recalibrate the society towards equality, to build communal relationships and to ensure that everyone had food, housing and other necessities. Coins, if you had enough, could buy you anything, if not in your community then in the next one. This was a new kind of freedom. This was also the time when the world would change dramatically, from Greece through to India and China, everything would change.

7

THE SINGULARITY

The Bronze Age Collapse involved not only Mycenaean Greece and the New Kingdom of Egypt but also the Hittite Empire in modern-day Turkey. In the void left by the Hittites, and also in the lands farther east, numerous small societies formed, grew over time, then merged with others until, eventually, the great kingdoms of Lydia, Babylon and Medea were formed.

Ultimately, in about 530 BCE, all of these were absorbed by Cyrus the Great into the Achaemenid Persian Empire. Cyrus encouraged tolerance, allowing individual ethnicities to practice their own rituals and religions, and he also allowed them to be repatriated if they had previously been displaced.

Under the rule of Cyrus the Hebrews began to return to their land after the period of Babylonian exile. They then consolidated all their ideas and stories into the Torah, properly defining themselves as a nation by reference to the genealogy, laws and stories described in the five books of the Torah. It is highly likely though, that the newly created Judaism also incorporated ideas from the Persian religion, Zoroastrianism. Zoroaster, who was born in 660 BCE, grouped the earlier pantheon of gods of the region into two forces, the force of good and that of evil. Unlike earlier Hebrews who believed in a nameless, formless god, Zoroastrians believe in one, universal, transcendent and supreme creator god.

Cyrus is mentioned on numerous occasions in the Torah, including Isaiah, where he is referred to as the shepherd of God. The book of Ezra almost exclusively describes the return from exile and starts with Cyrus' decree:

> *In the first year of Cyrus king of Persia, in order to fulfil the word of the Lord spoken by Jeremiah, the Lord moved the heart of Cyrus king of Persia to make a proclamation throughout his realm and also to put it in writing:*
>
> *This is what Cyrus king of Persia says:*
>
> *'The Lord, the God of heaven, has given me all the kingdoms of the earth and he has appointed me to build a temple for him at Jerusalem in Judah. Any of his people among you may go … and build the temple of the Lord, the God of Israel and may their God be with them…'*
>
> ~Ezra 1: 1-3

It was under the rule of Cyrus' successor, Darius the Great, from 522 to 486 BCE, that the Persian Empire reached its greatest extent, stretching from the Greek city-states in the west to the Indus River and the Indian city-states in the east. It is estimated that 44 per cent of the world's population at the time lived in this empire, making it the largest empire by population percentage in history.

Darius pushed eastward, taking the Sind and Punjab regions and so extending the territory to include all the lands of modern-day Pakistan. This eastward push forced the cities on the other side of the Indus River (also known as the Sindhu River) to unite and defend their territory. The names 'India' and their religion 'Hindu' both originated at this time as a response the Persian wars. Indeed, the name 'Hindu' was coined by the Persians for the *people* who lived beyond the river Indus and did not originally refer to their religion.

The religious and philosophical debate that attempted to define India and Hinduism obviously didn't satisfy everyone. The prince of one kingdom, Siddhārtha Gautama abandoned his right to succeed his father on the throne so as to search for his own truth. Six years later at the age of 35, in about 528 BCE, he became the Buddha.

Darius and Gautama Buddha were contemporaries and both were opposed to the Hindu. Both were also Aryan. Both Zoroastrianism and Buddhism advocate that active participation in life through good deeds is necessary to ensure happiness and to keep chaos and evil at bay. Both religions were protests against the cruel practices of old Aryan religions. Amunugama in *The History of Ancient Aryan Tribes in Sri Lanka* argues that the religion of the Persians had much to do with the shaping of the doctrine of the Buddha. He also indicates that the followers of the Buddha received both material support and encouragement in the spreading of their doctrine.

It is also highly likely that Darius supported Gautama Buddha in the development of Buddhist cities and the magnificent irrigation systems in Sri Lanka. In contrast to Hindu India, Sri Lanka is now a primarily Buddhist nation as a result of an influx of the Aryan Persian Buddhists at that time.

Darius was an empire builder. He built or rebuilt numerous highways, generally along the many paths of the ancient Silk Road with the aim of significantly expanding trade. The highway linking Sardis, the former capital of Lydia, with Susa, the administrative capital of the empire, was called the Royal Road. Herodotus describes the king's messengers who used this and the other highways in the empire: "Neither rain, nor snow, nor heat nor gloom of night stays these couriers from the swift completion of their appointed rounds." Alan Ryan, in *On Politics: the History of Political Thought from Herodotus to the Present* describes this as a type of early postal service and suggests that the Achaemenid Persian Empire as "the prototype of the modern nation state."

These highways crossing and connecting the empire benefitted all citizens and, like the irrigation systems in Sri Lanka, were early examples of public infrastructure. Public works are one important parallel between this prototype and the modern nation state. Religious tolerance is a second parallel. The third commonality was the single currency. Darius introduced the 'daric' as the standard coin for the empire. As a result of the significant economic influence of the Persians, many of the peoples in surrounding regions accepted the daric as the international currency. A fourth factor uniting the citizens in the empire was the adoption of a common language; the language of choice was Aramaic, a Semitic language that was probably the most widely spoken language at the time. A fifth factor was the creation of the idea of nationalism, which encouraged citizens to consider themselves as part of something bigger. Herodotus again:

The sacrificer is not allowed to pray for blessings on himself alone, but he prays for the welfare of the king, and of the whole Persian people, among whom he is of necessity included.
                                    ~Herodotus, *The History*

I find it extraordinary that the Achaemenid Persians could have such a significant impact on the development of modern political, economic and religious ideas and yet have little more than cursory mention in Western high school history lessons.

Herodotus, the first investigative historian, explores the development of the Persian Empire in *The History* written in about 450 BCE as he tried to understand the origins of the Greco-Persian wars. He notes that, "the Persian nation is made up of many tribes. Those which Cyrus assembled and persuaded to revolt from the Medes were the principal ones on which all others are dependent."

It appears that Cyrus recognised that by offering the different tribes what they wanted he could gain power for himself. Undoubtedly the Hebrews fought for Cyrus against their Babylonian rulers in exchange for being repatriated once Babylon had been absorbed by the Persians. This strategy of offering the various tribes what they want in exchange for political support is not dissimilar to our modern form of government. In this way the general principal of tolerance becomes central to 'good' governance; let everyone practice what they want so long as they pay tribute.

Even the idea of paying tribute is transformed at this time. After absorbing the Medean Empire and prior to conquering the Babylonians, Cyrus turned his attention to Lydia. Herodotus tells us that the Lydians "were the first nation to introduce the use of gold and silver coin, and the first who sold goods by retail". The adoption of coins to facilitate trade was not just one more similarity with the modern nation state. Coins, or the idea of money, is the defining characteristic of the modern nation state in two important ways.

Firstly, it allows the paying of tribute to be transformed into taxation. Rather than a payment enforced by the strong at the threat of physical harm, taxation purports to be a contractual exchange, a social contract. In the Persian example, the king creates coins and then pays a standing army of soldiers who will maintain order and so provide a stable economic environment. The coins can then be paid to any citizen for their services to the soldiers. The more coins the king produces and gives to the soldiers, the greater and broader will be the market they create. In exchange all citizens will pay a portion of their income to the king, which he will invest, perhaps in the development of public infrastructure, but ultimately at his discretion for the 'good' of the nation. Coins create markets where they previously did not exist, which enables the levying of taxes. Coins also create the need for a police force and public servants as the means through which the currency is distributed.

The second defining idea created through the introduction of coins is that of public value, which is somewhat akin to the concept of nationalism mentioned above. The idea of public value had consequences for our understanding of both the physical and the spiritual worlds. The coin, in fact, created a philosophical dilemma: How can one thing have two values? At one level the coin was just a lump of metal that had a certain material value. Once it was stamped with the king's image it suddenly had some greater value. There is now a material value and what may be called a public value, the value attributed to it by the public.

This dilemma begins to be expressed through new ideas about the human soul. Up until this time the spirit would have been regarded as the essence of a person and so it had the same value as the physical person. The essence simply travelled to a different world after death. From this time onwards people begin to wonder about the *value* of the human soul and its *relative value* to the body. Does the human soul have greater value than the body because it is immortal?

What creates that greater value? With respect to coins it is the public trust in the king that he will accept this alternative value in the payment of taxes. This begs the question: Why trust in a king, can we not trust in the community of citizens? In Athens, outside the Lydian and the later Persian empires, there is no image of kings on the coins. From 500 BCE the owl is used, symbolising wisdom and illustrating that the citizens trusted in the wisdom of the community to provide that greater value, the community assets and public infrastructure that were shared by, and benefitted, all. This gives birth to the philosophical inquiry into different forms of government.

More questions beg to be answered. When we ask: 'Who has the power to create this greater economic value,' we begin a conversation about absolute power and creation and defining what has 'value' and what *is* value. In this context societies re-imagine the various religions to include concepts of absolute power and creation.

In differentiating between, and therefore separating, the physical value from the public value, we are distinguishing between the material world and some other abstract world, so more questions arise. Do we not need to understand the physical world, in order to appreciate its value? What is this ideal world? What is an ideal? What is an idea? Is the king the ideal to which each person should aspire? To what should we aspire? If the king creates value, is there a perfect king, in a perfect world who creates everything?

By the time of Aristotle, the tension between the material and spiritual worlds is firmly entrenched in Western thinking. Whereas Plato argued that the Truth could be discovered only in the ideal world, giving it superiority, Aristotle argued the opposite, that Truth could be found here, in the material world. Christianity, founded on the ideas of Plato, and Science, founded on the perspective of Aristotle, have been in tension ever since, each claiming superior value. Is it meaningful to compare things that are different to determine which has greater value? Can we not accept differences as simply differences? Differences in perspectives, in talents, in assets, can complement our own to add value to the 'whole'.

Coins didn't just create a philosophical dilemma, this line of questioning creates the project of philosophy.

§

Near Sardis, the former capital of Lydia, the Greek Ionian port cities, including Miletus, Samos and Ephesus, had already been absorbed into the Lydian empire in about 560 BCE and so now were part of the Persian empire.

Miletus produced three of the earliest Greek philosophers, Thales, Anaximander and Anaximenes, just prior to its absorption into Lydia. These 'natural philosophers' were early scientists because they tried to explain natural phenomena by observation rather than accepting events as acts of gods. In parallel with the dilemma created by coins the reader will recall that the Homeric epics had encouraged Greeks to pursue their destiny. This allowed individuals to take life into their own hands, to trust their own judgement and their own observations, giving birth to science.

Anaximander suggested that the source of all things was a substance he referred to as the 'limitless' or the 'uncreated'. This had a profound influence on the ideas of Pythagoras, who in turn influenced Plato's conception of the 'ideal world'. Plato's ideas were then used to describe ideas central to Christianity, including the idea of a limitless and uncreated god, who was the source of all things and who lived in heaven, an ideal world.

Pythagoras, known for the mathematical theorem that bears his name, was born in Samos, another Ionian city. The Pythagorean theorem, though, is known to have been previously used by the Babylonians and Indians. Pythagoras also established a belief system called 'Pythagoreanism', which was rooted in mathematical and scientific pursuits because he believed that contemplation about the world was the greatest virtue, an idea that later fed into Plato's 'philosopher-kings' in *The Republic*. Plato argued that if contemplation is the greatest virtue, then the philosophers who contemplate are the most likely to govern justly.

For Pythagoras, this contemplation aimed at understanding the world was driven by the spiritual desire to free oneself from the endless cycle of birth and death. This is, of course, identical to the idea that freedom from the endless cycle of birth and death can be achieved by following the Buddhist Path— although the former seeks this through contemplation while the latter empties the mind through meditation. There is only a seven-year age difference between Pythagoras and Siddhārtha Gautama Buddha so there is no doubt that the Persian trade routes played a significant role in the sharing of these ideas across the Eurasian continents.

In mainland Greece, the battles of Marathon, in 490 BCE, and Salamis in 480 BCE, against Darius and his successor Xerxes, respectively, are considered to be amongst the most significant points in early European history. The second victory against the Persians ushered in the Classical period of Greek Antiquity, the rebuilding of the Parthenon, the explosion of art and creativity and, eventually, the philosophy of Socrates, Plato and Aristotle.

The great highways that now linked all parts of the empire, facilitated not only trade but also governance and education. The school of Athens could learn from the school in Taxila, in the Upper Indus River valley, and likely many others throughout Eurasia. It is no accident that this empire had a major impact on the philosophy, religion and economics of the time, both within and outside its borders.

It is also difficult to imagine that these travelling ideas did not also impact on or learn from China, as it too was connected into the network of highways. We also know that Confucius, who was born in 551 BCE, would have been teaching during the reign of Darius in a period of Chinese philosophical enquiry known as the 'hundred schools of thought'.

§

The most important effect of this first sample of globalisation was its impact on knowledge. The highways must have been magnificent, the armies awe-inspiring, the consolidated wealth of Darius extraordinary, but none of this matters today. The legacy of this period is the amazing spread and sharing of ideas across the Eurasian continent. Although they were built to facilitate trade, the highways, together with the new coinage, provided freedom for individuals to travel and share ideas.

Whenever these trade-based empires are created, an even greater empire of knowledge and ideas will be created. Although the Persians controlled nearly half of the known world's population, the connections forged through trade created an even greater empire of shared knowledge and ideas that also included India, China and the Greek-speaking world. Trade requires that people travel, not only to exchange goods but also to push new boundaries and explore new places, sometimes to develop new markets but also to learn from different cultures. Initially, when travelling, we tend to notice the differences but, eventually, we begin to appreciate our common humanity and recognise that we have more commonalities than differences. This is what generates a singular, human consciousness and that is why I have called this chapter 'The Singularity'.

The Achaemenids and numerous subsequent empires have come and gone, but the knowledge and ideas of that time endure. These ideas made a significant contribution to our present understanding of the world and so helped to form the economic, religious and political foundations of our cities as we imagine them today.

Yet much has been learnt and much has changed in the last 2,500 years since those foundations were built. In particular, our scientific understanding of the world, its natural systems and its place in the universe dramatically alters some of the ideas proposed at the time.

§

In the first seven chapters we travelled from the life of the fictional Ayla, who was raised by Neanderthals, to Moses, Homer, Cyrus, Darius, Buddha, Confucius, Pythagoras, Plato and Aristotle. In the next seven chapters I'd like to pull some of the key ideas together in order to explore specific themes as they relate to Cities. By developing these more fully I hope to make them relevant and applicable in the modern world.

Each of these specific themes, to be explored in subsequent chapters, will examine the various elements, or central Truths, that I believe are important to the development of a City.

The first theme relates to the scale of a City. I have indicated that the small, clan-sized societies of 25,000 years ago functioned democratically and all the citizens who were willing and able to participate did so. For these communities the 'whole' City consisted of no more than 30 or maybe 40 individuals.

When we compare this with the Persian Achaemenid Empire, in which case the 'whole' consists of many millions, it is difficult to imagine anything like this form of participation, and so its structure as a monarchy is understandable. Despite its characterisation as the prototype of the modern nation-state—tolerant, secular, with public infrastructure and services and focused on economic growth—we describe *our* states as democratic. This raises some obvious questions.

What is democracy and how much participation does it require? What is the difference between participatory democracy and representative democracy? What is the relationship between economics and democracy?

These questions will be explored in Chapter 8, 'Renaissance of the Polis', which traces through 3,000 years of Greek history to describe the origins of representative democracy and the effect on democracy of economic growth. From the 'Dark Ages' that followed the Bronze Age collapse, through Archaic then Classical Greece, and on to the modern era, this chapter describes how economic growth causes both geographic expansion and population growth. As the scale grows and individuals are no longer connected to each other, freedom, spirituality and creativity are converted into organised religion and a demand for productivity and further growth. Consequently, societies move through economic cycles starting from small collectives, through city-states, then into nation-states and finally globalised economies. Yet as the population increases, the voice of the individual, and therefore democracy, diminishes. The premise is that there are two mutually exclusive options for a society; economic growth or democratic effectiveness.

It is this alienation from their own government that ultimately brings these global economies to the precipice of collapse, and environmental failures push them over the edge. Considering that our own societies are standing at this same precipice, we need to consider: What decisions have been made in the past? Is collapse inevitable or is it possible for a society to transform itself?

In Chapter 9, 'Transparency, Democracy, Liberty', I explore the interesting phenomenon that as the Persian Empire reached its greatest extent under Darius the Great and became the pre-eminent and unchallenged international force, societies also experienced an unprecedented growth in philosophical enquiry. Both in India and in Greece, peoples impacted by the empire but outside of it were questioning the way in which the world works and asking what it means to live a 'good' life.

The evidence seems to suggest that the construction of highways for the purpose of trade also provided an effective avenue for the sharing of ideas. Was this a unique event or the beginning of a pattern? What is the impact of transparency and the free sharing of ideas on cities and societies?

In Chapter 10, 'From Infinity to Eternity', I discuss the story of fate versus destiny in more detail. In the opening chapter I suggested that we are bound to our fate unless we pursue our destiny. That is, either we accept our share of the 'whole', distributed unequally as it is—more for some, much less for others—or we can pursue a future in which we regard each other as equals. The desire for this shift has been the central ambition for some of the greatest figures in human history. Who were they, what change did they want and what did they mean by eternity?

In Chapter 11, 'The Theory of Everything', I explore the consequences of the ideas of Plato that argue that the soul has greater value than the body. Plato's ideas are based on the notion that everything aspires towards perfection, towards the perfect ideal. He suggests that those closer to this ideal are more perfect and therefore superior. In this construct the natural order is hierarchical. Is it 'natural' that our society should be hierarchical or could we imagine a society that strives for equality for all?

In Chapter 12, 'The Ecstasy of Yang', I contrast the nomadic or travelling lifestyle with the stable, place-based lifestyle. I have mentioned that the Agricultural Revolution introduced a second way of looking at the world; one that was based on anchoring oneself to a place, while the pre-existing lifestyle was nomadic. I introduced a number of examples to illustrate the importance of travel: the fictional Jondalar and his journey of discovery and the introduction of coinage, which offered the freedom to travel from community to community just to see and appreciate how others live and how the world works.

The idea of 'Yang' illustrates that although some prefer safety, stability, certainty and to be anchored to a home and job, others prefer to take risks, to be spontaneous and to push themselves to the edge. By reference to the Chinese concept of Yin and Yang, I suggest that Cities should be understood as a combination of complementary opposites. That is, Cities would be more efficient if they supported both the life of stability and safety as well as more nomadic options.

I have also mentioned that rather than trying to conquer nature, we should regard ourselves as stewards of nature and that we should live in harmony with nature. In Chapter 13, 'The Rhythm of Life', I ask: What does it mean to live in harmony with nature? This question is particularly important because, from the time humans domesticated animals and built their own housing rather than living in caves, we have been altering nature to suit our needs. So it is unlikely that living in harmony with nature can mean not changing the natural environment, so what *does* it mean? The contrast in this chapter relates to work. Must we build cities that demand more and more work or can we build Cities that resonate with the natural environment and so are able to work for us?

Throughout, I have argued that by putting limits on the economy, it is possible to create freedom. I indicated, though, that it is not just about putting limits on the economy but how you establish those limits. In the concluding Chapter 14, 'Fencing the Economy' I draw together all the ideas through which we could place limits on the economy, or operate the economy more efficiently, to create the time and space for the freedom that will permit creativity, spirituality, relaxation, enjoyment and the pursuit of destiny.

8

RENAISSANCE OF THE POLIS

With the collapse of the Mycenaean empire by about 1150 BCE, the epic age described by Homer—the empire that launched a thousand ships—ended, and Greece fell into what archaeologists refer to as the 'Dark Ages'. Little is known of this period but, for the following three centuries, there were extensive migrations across and within Europe. The rugged geography of Greece may have been partly responsible for the establishment of many small and independent city-states but the economic and political conditions should not be understated. In *The Mediterranean of the Ancient World*, Fernand Braudel compares the "extraordinary flowering of the Greek city-states … [with] the Italian cities of the Renaissance" and suggests that "the appearance of such autonomous urban centres is only conceivable in the absence of large-scale territorial states, which have gargantuan appetites for conquest. The Italian cities in their prime in the fourteenth century AD would have been unimaginable without the great recessions of the Middle Ages…".

During the eighth century BCE, as social groups increased in size, Greek society underwent dramatic changes as wealthy landowners started to appreciate some of the advantages of urbanisation. Urbanisation is the continuation of the process by which, through greater efficiency in the provision of foods, fewer people are required to provide supplies necessary for the whole population. The remainder began to concentrate in towns whose political and economic power slowly increased. The *agora* or 'marketplace' became the centre for meetings and jurisdiction as well as a place for worship and trading. Slowly, non-nobles and then artisans and other professionals followed and grew in number. To ensure that the governance of these compact states remained manageable and sustainable, especially with regard to food supply, population growth was managed by establishing independent colonies or trading-partner sister-states, rather than expanding, or sprawling, the city.

The city-state or *polis* was a fully self-sufficient entity, incorporating both the town and the countryside whose agriculture supported it. Entirely isolated, each polis became self-reliant. As a consequence, citizens enjoyed self-determination while the relatively compact form allowed the citizens to participate in the decision-making. It was in this environment of vigorous independence that a variety of legal systems flourished in the city-states of Greece. The legal and political systems were also structured, through their constitutions, so as to encourage the participation of the citizenry. This participation is the true essence of democracy.

From about the eighth century BCE, some three centuries before the Golden Age or Classical Age of Athens, many of the city-states that were principally Dorian in ethnicity were using a common constitution. There were as many as a hundred Dorian city-states in Crete and many similar states in the Peloponnese, the southern part of Greece.

In the Peloponnese—the modern day region of Laconia, from which we derive the word 'laconic'—the Spartan people adopted the Dorian system, which was communal in character, that is, there were no individual or private property rights. Citizens formally gave up their affiliations to family, ethnic groups and brotherhoods and extended their loyalty to the City alone. All possessions were held in common ownership, and even the citizens were given up by their families at the age of seven to begin their communal education and to ultimately serve in the army and then the polis collective. The people chose a frugal, 'spartan', lifestyle—minimalists even in their language, entirely consistent with their laconic nature.

The people of Athens were probably much more extroverted, and oratory was considered the supreme talent. Rhetoric and the ability to convince others ultimately led to the development of today's parliamentary system, the only purpose of which appears to be the rhetoric. As our modern systems are derived from this model, the expression 'parliament', which means 'speaking place' appears accurate. Before rhetoric came to define the parliament the original purpose of the 'gathering at the agora' was to achieve outcomes for the common good according to the will of the people. The Greek word for parliament is '*βουλή*' (pronounced 'voul-ee'), which means 'will', that is, to enact 'the will of the citizens'.

These two extremes, the Spartan introverts—laconic, minimalist and communal—and the Athenian extroverts—gregarious, confident and dominating—illustrate the two extremes in human nature and provide a metaphor for the socialist versus capitalist extremes in our own political structures.

The so-called 'Golden Age' of Athens, which many suggest formed the basis of Western civilisation, was dominated politically by one man. Pericles led 'democratic' Athens for thirty-two years. He was instrumental in the ostracism from the city of his major competition. It could be said that he was a benevolent dictator who allowed creativity to flourish, but it is difficult to suggest that he was democratic. The historian Thucydides, a contemporary of Pericles, summarised his leadership in one famous sentence: "It was in name a democracy but in fact the rule by the archon [ruler or lord]".

With the earlier introduction of the Council of Four Hundred, which became the first representative parliament, the flavour had begun to shift from citizen participation to citizen representation. Clearly, as Athens grew beyond the scale of other city-states, participatory democracy was no longer feasible. It appears that their rhetoric allowed Athenians to convince themselves, and future generations, that representative democracy still provided the same power to its citizens as did participatory democracy.

Athens, therefore introduced 'representative parliamentary democracy' rather than democracy in its fuller participatory sense, which, of course, already existed. In my opinion then, the most accurate characterisation of the political legacy of Athens is the introduction of rhetoric as a means of destroying participatory democracy.

Although the Spartan version of the Dorian constitutional system was also not a perfect democracy, it certainly predated by at least a century the Athenian constitution prepared by Solon, who was referred to by Aristotle as "the *first* champion of the people". In each case, the people who were deemed to be citizens gathered in the *agora* and established a system of rule. Those who were strongest, or wealthiest, would have driven the discussion that ultimately led to the reinforcement of their power and privilege. The Dorian constitution, although providing leadership by hereditary kingship, also included ten annually elected magistrates and a council of thirty elders, all of whom were elected by the Assembly of citizens. Aristotle suggests that: "this body [the Assembly] has no power to do anything except vote assent to measures decided upon by the Elders". Nevertheless, this is more substantial than the voting rights of citizens today in our Western representative democracies, who do not have the right to vote on specific laws at all.

It should be noted that the Dorian system of government appears to have been most stable in Crete, where the constitution persisted unchanged until the third century. Apparently the very large number of relatively small similar-sized states acted as a deterrent to the expansion of any one state. Perhaps this is how we can imagine our future—as an integrated network of self-sufficient, self-determining city-states.

A number of conclusions can be drawn from this discussion with respect to the balance between democracy and economic growth and the configuration of cities. Firstly, the Greeks originally regarded democracy as a mechanism for participation and civic responsibility. The Ephebic Oath—the Athenian oath of allegiance—included an expectation that citizens would "strive increasingly to quicken the public's sense of civic duty" and thus "transmit this City, not only not lesser, but greater and more beautiful than it was transmitted to us." This engendered a communal atmosphere, as did the communal property ownership system in the Dorian communities. The self-interest that is at the core of a capitalist system is at odds with the selflessness demanded by the negotiation of agreements for the public good that is central to democracy.

Secondly, democracy is more workable in small rather than large communities. In fact, democracy is inconsistent with large cities or nation-states where citizens can be lost in impersonal alternative collective networks. It is clear that, eventually, Athens became a victim of its own economic success. By attracting more and more people, the contribution of each citizen was diluted. As the citizens' power is lost, the few with authority—the oligarchy, which literally means the government by the few—are more able to pursue their own private agenda. This becomes a self-feeding loop as the wealthy enact laws that benefit themselves, increasing both their wealth and their authority. Until this expansion of Athens, essentially for the obvious objective of increasing its power relative to other cities, city-states managed their populations by establishing new sister cities as trading partners.

Finally, the above discussion illustrates that a sense of community is fostered when attention is focused on the community itself and not in the expansion or the control of other communities.

§

In the seventh century BCE, Athens was in turmoil. In about 620 BCE the law-maker Draco had introduced the first written laws, making them known to all literate citizens. The laws provided that they could be enforced only by a court of citizens. Draco also introduced the 'Council of Four Hundred', which was later to become the representative parliament. The Draconian laws enshrined earlier oral laws and, in a society where status was determined by wealth, the new laws also provided that if any person did not repay a debt to a citizen of higher status, that person would be thrown into slavery. This did not apply if the debt was owed to a person of lower status, so this inevitably created a serious division in the society between rich and poor, reducing most of the population to serfdom or slavery and ensuring that, according to Aristotle's *The Athenian Constitution*, "the land was in the hands of a few".

When Plato wrote *The Republic*, he clearly drew from the Athenian experience of this period in his review of 'Imperfect Societies'. His assessment of how an oligarchy changes into democracy has striking similarities with our world today:

> *Then doesn't oligarchy change into democracy ... as a result of lack of restraint in the pursuit of its objective of getting as rich as possible? ...*

Because the rulers, owing their power to wealth as they do, are unwilling to curtail the extravagance of the young and prevent them squandering money and ruining themselves; for it is by loans to such spendthrifts or by buying up their property that they hope to increase their own wealth and influence. …

It should then be clear that love of money and adequate self-discipline in its citizens are two things that cannot co-exist in any society; one or the other must be neglected. …

This neglect and encouragement of extravagance in an oligarchy often reduces to poverty men born for better things. …

Some of them are in debt, some disenfranchised, some both, and they settle down, armed with their stings, and with hatred in their hearts, to plot against those who have deprived them of their property, and against the rest of society, and to long for revolution. …

Meanwhile the money-makers, bent on their business, don't appear to notice them, but continue to inject their poisoned loans wherever they can find a victim and to demand high rates of interest on the sum lent, with the result that the drones and beggars multiply. …

Yet even when the evil becomes flagrant they will do nothing to quench it [such as by introducing] suitable legislation … [for example] If contracts for a loan were, in general, made by law at the lender's risk, there would be a good deal less shameless money-making and a good deal less of the evils I have been describing. …

But as the oligarchs reduce their subjects to the state we have described, while as for themselves live in luxury and idleness, physical and mental, become idle, and lose their ability to resist pain or pleasure. …

And they themselves care for nothing but making money,
and have no greater concern for excellence than the poor. …
Then democracy originates when the poor win, kill or
exile their opponents, and give the rest equal civil rights and
opportunities of office, appointment to office being, as a rule,
by lot. …

These words are a Truth in our times too. Those of us to whom fate was generous, who live in luxury and idleness, are generally oblivious to the plights of others. Some even see it as a game to "inject their poisoned loans wherever they can find a victim".

In *Voltaire's Bastards: The Dictatorship of Reason in the West*, John Ralston Saul argues that this transition from oligarchy to democracy can occur violently, by revolution, as occurred with the French and American Revolutions, or it can occur with relatively little bloodshed, as it did in Athens.

So how did this transition occur? As a result of the relatively small scale of the community, the individual voice was louder in Athens than it was in France or in the Americas. The wealthy had nowhere to hide. The physical proximity between the rich and the disenfranchised in the compact polis meant that the poor had to be heard. They spoke most eloquently through the poet Solon who continually criticised the rich. The inherent flexibility in the governance of the compact community allowed the poet to be elevated to ruler with full powers, illustrating the flexibility of a participatory democracy, which is able to change its form and government style in response to the circumstances of the day.

Indeed, this episode appears to have triggered in the minds of Athenians that anyone, not just aristocrats, was entitled to govern. The term 'tyrant' originated in this period, and, in

Greek, the word carried no implication as to the character of the person, it simply meant 'sovereign' or 'master'. Tyrants would often gain popularity by siding with 'the people' against 'the elite', a strategy previously adopted by Cyrus the Great in forming the Achaemenid Persian Empire.

So how did the poet Solon exercise his powers? His first act was to repeal the Draconian laws, free all enslaved citizens and redeem all forfeited lands. Essentially, he cancelled all debts. The reform was known as *seisachtheia* or 'the shaking off of the burdens' and was similar to the debt jubilees previously practised in Sumeria and Mesopotamia, which are also referred to in Deuteronomy 15.

The Ancient Greek word *seisas* means to 'move' or 'shake' violently, as in an earthquake. The word *achthos* means 'burden' or 'weight' and is applied equally to physical, spiritual and emotional weights. A debt was regarded as a physical, spiritual and emotional weight.

By shaking off the burdens Solon liberated both the land and those tied to it. In *The Athenian Constitution*, Aristotle notes:

> *The following seem to be the three most democratic features of Solon's constitution: The ban on loans on the security of the person; next, permission for anyone who wished to seek retribution for those who were wronged; and third, the one which is said particularly to have contributed to the power of the masses, the right of appeal to the jury-court—for when the people are masters of the vote they are masters of the state.*

An important consequence of these reforms was the concept of 'standing' in modern legal terminology. The masses, as

Aristotle calls them, finally had real value in the eyes of the law. They had the right to 'stand' in the courts. They had the right of appeal, any person had the right to seek retribution for any other person and indebtedness could no longer result in a loss of liberty. Importantly, the legal reforms would have been completely meaningless without the cancelling of debts that freed the people from their economic burden. The right to access the courts would have been worthless to an indebted servant. The reforms of Solon illustrate that economic and political freedoms are inextricably linked and perhaps simply different sides of the same coin.

This created a dramatic shift in the balance of power and although, as Aristotle writes "the city continued in a state of turmoil" for nearly a century, the shift could not be reversed. The aristocrats continued to wield the power, but when it came to determining who amongst them would govern, it was usually the one who offered further reforms that increased the standing of the masses. Athens was thus set on a path to a representative democracy in which citizens were granted a broad range of rights.

As a result of the reforms of Solon, it was no longer inevitable that a city must be governed unilaterally by one or a few individuals but could instead be governed more broadly and by negotiation. Traditional clan- and village-scale communities had always been governed democratically, as this is the natural human inclination, but as the community increased to the city scale, which at this time meant several thousand citizens, power became concentrated amongst the few who referred to themselves as aristocrats.

Government systems were now seen as sitting along a continuum from monarchy—literally a single ruler—through oligarchy—government by the few—to democracy, where *all* citizens hold power. It was now possible to discuss and debate different systems of government along this continuum, and citizens recognised that broadening access to government was possible. By reference to this continuum, it is also possible to appreciate that a representative democracy is still effectively an oligarchy and a long way from the point at which all citizens have the opportunity to speak and be heard.

An assessment of whether a society is democratic should consider where it is located on this continuum, by asking what proportion of the citizens can meaningfully contribute to decisions and agreements. This assessment, though, should not be used to compare one system, or City, with another. Where a City sits on the continuum is only a snapshot of its present conditions. Citizens should be asking themselves: In which direction is our City heading? Are we striving towards greater democracy and participation or less? For example, if we are advocating further population growth will this increase or diminish the voice of the individual? Are we each participating in the public debates, or are we sitting back and allowing ourselves to be 'governed'? Is our society structured in such a way that all voices can be heard?

So the reforms of Solon diminished the wealth of the rich and increased the wealth of the poor, driving the City towards greater equality. Despite the ongoing struggle and instability, this sense of equality, freedom to participate and confidence grew and peaked with the explosion of energy and creativity that was the Golden Age of Athens. It is not unreasonable to suggest that the Classical Era could in large part be attributed to the rule of a poet-dictator who undermined the land- and property-ownership system by cancelling all debts.

§

The current economic circumstances faced by the West, and specifically the sovereign crises in several nations, including Greece, since 2010, are extraordinarily similar to those of sixth century Athens. Any awareness of its own history should clearly prohibit Athens, now the Greek capital, from accepting a greater debt burden from the European Union. Austerity measures are actions aimed at reducing public goods and services in one country to guarantee the servicing of private debts. These debts are private debts because the creditors are private banks and the debtors are a small group of aristocrats and not the general public of Greece, who had no part in the management of these government finances. Similarly, stimulus packages simply increase the public debt burden so as to stimulate private commerce. Strategies could instead be geared towards the opposite agenda of cancelling debts, public as well as private.

It is no coincidence that the principal theme of the discussions surrounding the economic stability of Greece, and other southern European 'Club Med' states, relates to the need for them to change their ways, their attitudes, perhaps their values. Greeks do not value property in the Western manner and do not seek to spend their lives growing their assets. The reference to 'Club Med' itself suggests that these peoples are enjoying their lives too much and should instead tie themselves to the mantra of economic growth for its own sake, supported by growing personal, corporate and national debt.

The key point is that Greeks have traditionally held a different view of the role of a citizen in society, had different expectations of the purpose of government, and have recognised the impacts that the self-interest required in the pursuit of money has on a society. Put simply, the Western system, based on economic growth, suggests that size matters. Larger government wields more power on the world stage, bigger debt leverages more assets and greater or faster growth accelerates access to wealth (for the few oligarchs). The example of the participation and flexibility of a small *polis* suggests that in fact size does matter, and small is beautiful.

Rather than seeking growth, the Greeks sought moderation and balance. This striving towards moderation is identical to the Buddhist idea of striving towards a Middle Way—that is, away from extreme self-indulgence and extreme asceticism. At the same historical period as the Greek and Buddhist thinkers, Confucius also taught the 'Doctrine of the Mean', that 'excess' is similar to 'deficiency' and that the goal should be to maintain balance and harmony by directing the mind to a state of constant equilibrium.

In *The Republic*, Plato seeks to identify an ideal state and suggests that it would have characteristics similar to those of an ideal person. These characteristics or cardinal virtues are:

wisdom, or mastery over the mind; courage, the mastery of the spirit; and self-discipline, which is the mastery over the body. The fourth characteristic is justice. A significant portion of *The Republic* is simply an attempt to discover the meaning of justice. In the dialogue, Socrates suggests that justice sustains and perfects the other three cardinal virtues.

> *The just man will not allow the three elements which make up his inward self to trespass on each others functions or interfere with each other but by keeping all three in tune, like the notes of a scale ... [he] will in the truest sense set his house to rights, attain self-mastery and order, and live on good terms with himself. When he has bound these elements into a disciplined and harmonious whole, and so become fully one instead of many...*

Justice is a cultivated sense of moderation and balance. To the Greeks, anything in excess was evil, even excessive wisdom, courage or self-discipline. Justice reflects the choices and actions of the person or city or society. According to the Greeks, the material excess required by capitalism is inconsistent with the qualities of a just man or a just City, as it would represent a satisfaction of appetite at the expense of mental and spiritual growth. The aim was harmony, to bind the many into a disciplined and harmonious whole.

§

In 338 BCE, ten years after the death of Plato, the Greek city-states fell under Macedonian rule, and Europe commenced a period of almost continual instability as the various powers struggled for supremacy. The Hellenistic period began with the aggressive campaigns of Alexander the Great, in which he conquered the entire Persian Achaemenid Empire. After his death in 323 BCE, his Eurasian empire was divided into four, and the nationalist campaigns that followed also included the Syrians, the Carthaginians, who dominated most of northern Africa and southern Spain, and, of course, Rome. This period saw the end of the city-states as imperialist and nationalist forces took advantage of the growing prosperity and sought to gain more land and wealth.

By about 27 BCE, the general supremacy of Rome was established and Caesar Augustus established the Pax Romana, or Roman Peace, which continued to about 280 AD.

Fernand Braudel writes: "The Mediterranean became a calmer place, lulled into somnolence by the benefits and dangers of the 'heavy uniformity of the Pax Romana.'" The principal purpose of the Pax Romana was to allow free movement and trade for Roman citizens throughout the empire. The freedom of movement allowed a greater sharing of ideas, and Greek-speaking Roman citizens like Paul of Tarsus took full advantage, supporting the formation of independent, self-sustaining communities in a number of cities. The community assembly was called the *ecclesia*, the same word used by the citizens of Classical Athens for their legislative assembly. These communities advocated selflessness and the sharing of possessions rather than the love of money. They sought to focus on self-development and the development of a communal society based on love for one's neighbour.

There are many similarities between the period leading to the early Christian communities and a more recent period of Western European history, closer to our Modern Age. Empires collapsed, and an extended period known as the Dark Ages commenced. Out of the gloom, as economic prosperity grew and trade began, more people were able to leave agriculture and gather in towns. By gathering and joining forces, working collectively, their prosperity multiplied. The Greek city-states and the Italian cities of the Renaissance both reflect this period where the wealth translated into significant development in all areas of human endeavour. In each case, wealth changed the political landscape.

In the final heartbeat of its democratic period, Athens was dominated by Pericles, as the Medici family dominated Florence. The period of benevolent dictators is the idealised pinnacle and the beginning of the economic bubble. Greater wealth significantly expanded trade, and the size and power of the merchant class grew. This economic prosperity spread and had the same effect in many states. The city-states challenge each other for supremacy, alliances were forged and, eventually, empires formed. As they grew, border disputes occurred as empires collided. Eventually, very strong individuals rose to power. Alexander was a superior leader from Macedonia, the periphery of Classical Greece, who believed he could master the super-powers of the time—the major Greek states and the Persian Achaemenid Empire. Napoleon was a superior leader from Corsica, the periphery of Enlightenment Europe who believed that he could master all of the major European powers of his time. Both Alexander and Napoleon conquered Europe quickly, only for their empires to quickly disintegrate, leaving an environment of instability. The Hellenistic period, until the establishment of the Pax Romana, has many similarities with the nationalistic period through the late 18th, 19th and early 20th centuries, until the establishment of the United Nations after the Second World War and the Pax Americana ostensibly brought a controlled peace to the world ... to ensure the continuation of trade.

It was in the nationalistic environment, when maps and national boundaries were continually redrawn, that the nation of Modern Greece was established in 1821. In the context of a romantic rediscovery of Classical Greece, the various nationalist European Powers and Russia noted the slow decay of the Ottoman Empire. Part of Europe was up for grabs ... but let's not get ahead of ourselves!

§

Braudel argues that the success of Rome was founded on the simple principle of tolerance. Rome tolerated the practices of its peoples, making it easier to assimilate a culturally diverse population. This was an almost exact replica of the strategy of Cyrus the Great in establishing the Persian Empire.

This idea of tolerance did not sit comfortably with Greeks who had difficulty reaching any consensus amongst themselves let alone tolerating others. They coined the pejorative term 'barbarian' for non-Greeks. Democracy itself is likely to arise only amongst peoples who, individually and collectively, consider that no one else could be superior to them.

Tolerance, though, is a double-edged sword. Tolerance allows the replacement of justice with compliance and enforcement of the law. Rather than struggling to find justice within themselves and so to create a city of similar character, as was the way of the Greeks, the Romans simply defined justice by writing the law. Rather than enquiring and searching for beauty and the Middle Way, the Romans required conformity and compliance. Whereas the Greek goddess of justice, 'Dike', (which means justice), stood with her sisters 'Irene' (peace) and 'Eunomia' (good order) as guardians of the gates of heaven, the Roman goddess 'Justitia' now stands alone, blindfolded and holding a sword—a symbol of the Supreme Court of the United States. The blindfold symbolises tolerance—that all are treated equitably under the law—while the sword depicts enforcement.

Equity *beneath* the law, that is, being treated fairly, should not be confused with equality. Someone is the author of the law, someone who claims to know good and evil, so equity beneath the law is equity beneath the authors of the law. Equality relates to equal standing of *all* citizens, which, therefore, requires the absence of a superior authority. It is an environment in which justice is discovered when the opening words on all sides are: "I see you".

This 'tolerance' is the principal expression of a secular state, which is central to the Western system of government. It allowed the Romans to adopt the various Bronze Age Greek gods as their state religion but also permitted the practice by its constituent cultures of their own religions. In this context, Christianity was allowed to be practiced freely. According to Charles Freeman's *The Closing of the Western Mind: The Rise of Faith and the Fall of Reason,* it was only when Christians did not comply with Roman law that they found themselves in conflict with it.

Indeed, it was not until 250 AD, when the number of Christians had swelled to the point where they compromised the empire that persecutions commenced in earnest. Even so, the objective of the edict issued by the emperor Decius was, in an empire in decline, to restore traditional cults so as to win back the favour of the gods. It was not a persecution against the beliefs of the Christians but, rather, a strategy targeted at changing their collaborative and communal systems, which so dramatically impacted on the economy of the empire.

In 274 AD the Roman emperor Aurelian officially recognised a Syrian religion that worshipped the sun god. 'Sol Invictus', which means 'The Unconquered Sun', now held equal status with the traditional Roman gods. Roman coins of this time depict the emperor wearing a 'solar crown' on one side, while the sun god wore the same crown on the other.

This period is particularly important in the study of law and government. Roman tolerance had allowed the empire to agglomerate all of Europe, the Middle East and North Africa. The Pax Romana had been in place for some time, and trade continued under the protection of the army. The legal framework of Roman law had allowed the empire to grow, but its ongoing management was becoming more and more difficult. Indeed the Roman legal system was designed around the principle of economic growth, which has little to contribute to the management of people and natural resources.

The collapse of the empire was imminent, and an exceptional individual was needed. Diocletian, a remarkable organiser and statesman, became emperor in 284 AD. He introduced the idea of 'delegated power', appointing a co-emperor, dividing the empire in two, each led by rulers with the title 'Augustus' and supported by an appointed deputy called 'Caesar'. The 'Tetrarchy', or 'rule of four', allowed more effective responses to attacks, and a string of military victories followed. The empire was divided into smaller provinces, and tax collection was taken out of the hands of the military with the appointment of civilian governors. Land was assessed according to its productivity and a fixed sum levied. All the elements of institutional government were now in place. Freeman argues that "for the first time it was possible for there to be an imperial budget and even some elementary long term planning". Diocletian significantly advanced the conversion of the Roman Empire into a bureaucratic and institutionalised government.

When the four emperors were fighting wars, looking outward, considering growth, there were few problems. When they were managing the one empire, four leaders seemed not to work so well. A strong general named Constantine took control. Having held the position of Caesar from 306 AD and Augustus of the West from 312 AD, he took control of the whole empire in 324 AD, ending the 'Civil Wars of the Tetrarchy'. Politically shrewd and ambitious, Constantine continued to employ the Roman idea of 'tolerance' as he appreciated the power of religion and the ability to unify by finding commonalities. His predecessors had already embraced some Eastern ideas and Constantine continued to print coins that depicted him as the new Roman sun god, 'Sol Invictus'. He claimed to see a vision from the Greek sun god, Apollo, who promised him that he would rule for thirty years. Constantine also integrated the ideas of Plato who, in *Timaeus*, had described a god who was the Creator of the Universe and the perfect archetype or template for the 'imperfect' world. The god described by Plato was also part of a trinity that existed before the heavens, was unchanging and invisible, represented the ultimate 'Good', and was free of jealousy. He was the source of knowledge and the supreme truth.

In the battles of 312 AD, during the Civil War of the Tetrarchy, Constantine claimed that he had received support from "the supreme deity" apparently seeing a vision of a cross in the sky above the sun with the inscription, "By this sign, conquer". He marked his soldiers' shields

The Chi-Rho symbol with the 'Chi-Rho' symbol, an early version of the cross, depicting Christ as the banner for war.

In 321 AD Constantine instructed that all citizens, irrespective of faith, should be united in observing the 'venerable day of the sun', a day of rest and celebration of the Sun god, an idea that continues today as Sunday.

In 324 AD, after taking absolute control of the empire, Constantine relocated the capital to Byzantium, renaming it Constantinople. After nearly twenty years of civil wars he needed to provide some stability and resolving religious disputes and controversies was central to this strategy. The following year, 325 AD, he summoned the first General Ecumenical

Council of the Christian Church at Nicaea. The Nicene Creed is the codification of the Christian faith. Constantine, who had implemented and advanced many of the administrative reforms of Diocletian, institutionalised Christianity. By developing the idea of tolerance into a general absorption of ideas, Constantine had created a new society. The Byzantine Empire, which lasted for more than ten centuries, was primarily his construct. In the last days of the Roman Empire, he adopted Diocletian's institutionalisation of government, identified the sun as a common element in a range of religions in the empire, gave everyone a day of rest and used Platonic philosophy to illustrate that he sought peace, truth and the good of all.

The use of such logical and reasoned arguments was consistent with the eastern part of the empire, steeped as it was in the Greek philosophical tradition and the practice of rhetoric. The West, though, was now far removed from the centre of government. Latin was the primary language and so the West was also linguistically removed from the philosophical and religious debates of the empire, which were now conducted in Greek. For example, none of Plato's works was available in Latin until 321 AD when only the early parts of *Timaeus* were translated. Interestingly the translated sections were those that describe his idea of the Creator God, translated just in time, perhaps, for the concept to be used in formulating Christian doctrine in the Council of Nicaea.

In 395, the empire was divided again, essentially along these linguistic lines. Eventually, the Western empire collapsed and Europe's Dark Ages followed.

In the East, though, the Christian Byzantine Empire consolidated and grew. Through a series of Ecumenical Councils, the framework of Christian theology was formed, aligning the authority of the Church with that of the empire. The Councils also served to rule on 'heresies'. The word 'heresy' is derived from the Greek word for 'choice'. Through reasoned argumentation, generally coloured by political motives, those who did not conform were side-lined. Eventually, a 'Catholic Orthodox Church' was formed. Notably, the term 'orthodox' literally means 'correct opinion', while 'catholic' means 'all-embracing'. So if you made the right choice and conformed to the correct opinion you were embraced.

As with the West, the rule of the Church became absolute. Unlike the West, the Eastern Church was supported by the weight of the institutionalised governing structure of the state. All aspects of the life of the citizen were governed by the forces of conformity. In every church in every village, people were told of their failures and their sins. They were told of the consequences of making the wrong choice. Their reliance on the dispensations of Church and State were absolute.

By viewing human history in this broad-brush manner, it is possible to appreciate that as people and societies lose control of, or proximity to, their government, their dependence on external authority grows. Greek society, which a few centuries earlier had flourished in the city-states, had passed through the constant wars of the nationalistic Hellenistic period, the somnolence of the Pax Romana and, finally, to Christian institutionalised religion. Authority had passed from the level of the city, to the nation, then to the 'global empire' and, ultimately, people believed that authority lay beyond earth itself!

Essentially, we must make the social contracts that govern the way we interact. If we don't make these contracts ourselves, someone who is more distant will make them and impose them. If we believe that others live better than we do simply because they are wealthier, then we are inviting them to impose their laws. Making these social contracts requires us to focus on our own city's public goods, our collective, local interests. Our societies are currently forged on the principles of tolerance and self-interest. We have adopted the economist Adam Smith's suggestion that if we all look after our own self-interest, the 'invisible hand' will guide the market to provide all our needs, including common needs and care for our neighbours. There is no invisible hand or hand of God. Those who claim the existence of such hands do so in order to impose their will on others.

§

The divisions between East and West grew through events such as the Great Schism of 1054, when the Pope of Rome and the Patriarch of Constantinople mutually excommunicated each other, and the sack of Constantinople in 1204 by the Fourth Crusade.

The Ottoman Turks, primarily Muslims, took Constantinople in 1453. In 1454, Johann Gutenberg printed the Gutenberg Bible, the first mechanically printed book. The printing press was to become the single most important tool for challenging the authority of the Western Roman Catholic Church. Not until the advent of the internet would an invention so transform the social landscape by democratising access to knowledge and ideas. Suddenly, any person could spread a message without reference to the established authorities. In 1517, Martin Luther posted his 'Ninety-Five Theses' objecting to Church autocracy, and the Reformation began in earnest.

As the West passed through, or rather engaged in, the Renaissance, the Reformation, the scientific revolution, the Enlightenment and the French and Industrial Revolutions, each informing and reforming the various aspects of Western government, Greeks were governed by the Church. Whereas the West set aside theocracy, Greeks were required to submit to Church authority. The tolerant, secular state, the state based on reason rather than remote religious ideals, which is central to government in the West, arises from the historical path travelled by the West and contrasts starkly with the recent Greek journey.

In Greece, the Ottoman Turks, originally nomadic warriors, were faced with the same dilemma as the Romans after creating a huge empire. How do you govern a huge agglomeration of peoples and faiths? Whereas the Romans employed tolerance, the written law and enforcement, the Ottomans simply divided the empire into 'millets', or nations, on the basis of their faith. Besides the ruling Muslim millet, there was an Orthodox millet, a Catholic millet, a Jewish millet and others.

The rulers of these millets were the Church bishops who, under Byzantine rule, *shared* the government with the state authorities. They now held absolute power over all aspects of everyday life. According to Richard Clogg's *A Concise History of Greece,* people "had more dealings with their own religious authorities than with any Ottoman officialdom. ... The quid pro quo for the granting of such a high degree of communal autonomy was that the patriarch and the hierarchy were expected to act as guarantors of the loyalty of the Orthodox faithful to the Ottoman state."

With such a concentration of power in the church hierarchy, the competition for the higher offices was fierce. The obvious consequence of such competition is corruption, as many compete for the few high offices. The sultan's chief minister, the Grand Vezir became the recipient of substantial bribes, or 'peshkesh', every time the office of the patriarch changed hands, which he ensured happened often. To recoup this, bribes were required all the way down the chain. The church thus became entangled in the institutionalised corruption typical of the Ottoman system of rule. This institutionalised corruption persists in Greece to this day.

As is generally the case in such a regime, laws appear arbitrary but are essentially made to serve the private interests of those in power, including financial interests and enhancing their own power. The only way individuals could defend themselves against this capricious form of government was to secure the protection of a highly placed patron who would mediate on their behalf. After the Greek revolution of 1821 against the Ottoman Turks, when a dysfunctional constitutional government was implemented, parliamentary deputies filled the role of patrons and required, at election time, the support of those they had helped. The principal assistance that was offered, in a perpetually floundering economy, was work in the inflated public sector. Today, *'ρουσφέτι'* (pronounced 'roosfeti')—the reciprocal dispensation of favours—and *'μέσα'* (pronounced 'messa')—the connections that are useful—are the basic tools by which individuals in Greece are able to manage their daily lives.

Although the approach of the Ottomans was different from that of the Romans, their objectives were the same. Both sought to create a stable environment that was tolerant of different ideologies, religions and ways of living. The purpose of the stability was to create the optimal conditions for trade. By enhancing trade, growing the scale of the economy, they could increase the total amount they could collect in taxes. Just as in the earlier Persian Achaemenid Empire, increasing the territories and populations under their control also increased the economy and, consequently, the tax revenue.

Although religious tolerance appears to provide freedom for the individual in terms of personal beliefs, the perpetual focus on trade and economic growth, as well as the inevitable indebtedness of the majority of the population, allows little if any opportunity for real, meaningful spirituality or freedom.

§

For decades prior to the French Revolution, its people had engaged in extensive debates asking: Why can't we govern ourselves? Why do we need to rely on external authorities, such as the Church, to tell us how to manage our lives? These questions are the basis for the movement called Rationalism.

The formation of the city-states of the Renaissance and the Reformation of the Church in Europe are a result of the use of reason. This was the birth of the Age of Reason or, rather, it was its rebirth, as Homer had previously discarded the Bronze Age Olympian gods and advocated that people take their destiny into their own hands.

Rationalists argued that we can make laws for ourselves by applying basic common sense and moral values. The thought process that allows for the formation of a new state, or City, by deliberately discarding old ideas has been referred to as the 'project of autonomy'. This is what I mean by Rethinking the City.

There was no equivalent debate prior to the Greek Revolution in 1821. There was no 'idea' of Greece amongst the Greeks, only an adjustment of boundaries and a new authority in power. The Ottomans had dismantled the Byzantine state structure and, when they were defeated, the authority of the church structure also fell away.

At the time, the powerful monarchies of Europe and Russia were regularly renegotiating, frequently on the battlefield, the various boundaries of Europe. This was the nationalist period of world politics. The European Powers were linked through their aristocratic families; they shared a notional democratic government framework and, together with Russia, also shared the Christian religion. This set them apart from the Islamic Ottomans. Western Europeans romantically identified with Classical Greece as their cultural heritage and wanted to force out the Islamic Ottomans and form a Christian Greek State. The anti-Islamic, pro-Christian and pro-Classical Greece sentiments aligned, and the Greek nation was formed.

By 1823, a governing authority was established. By 1824, internal feuding had erupted into all out civil war. It took until 1832 to settle the borders of the new state. Greece was not a party to the agreement, which was negotiated between Britain, France and Russia on the one side and the Ottomans on the other. A seventeen-year-old Bavarian prince was appointed King of Greece. The European Powers assisted the Greek Revolution by granting numerous substantial loans. By keeping Greece indebted, they were able to impose their political will on the new state. Greece has been on the precipice of collapse ever since, defaulting on its loans in 1826, 1843, 1860, 1893 and 1932.

Greek merchants who had lived in other parts of Europe and had experienced the French debate wanted a modern Rationalist system. The 1844 constitution was based on imported French Human Rights principles. The bureaucrats who served the Ottomans wanted a return to the glories of Byzantium; their private interests were served by re-establishing pre-existing institutions. They forced the adoption of the Byzantine code, drafted in 1345, as the principal source of civil law.

The Greek nation commenced its journey indebted and divided. Rather than assembling to establish a system suitable to its present citizens, they adopted established structures and cemented a serious social division with which Greeks today are still struggling. Rather than working with their sparse natural resources to provide food and housing, the local interests of the citizens, they sought to import institutions that enhance the private interests of the few in authority.

Much can be said of twentieth-century Greece: the disastrous imperialist campaign of the 1920s, the huge influx of refugees that followed, the Great Depression of the 1930s, the Second World War, the ensuing civil war, the emigration of a generation through the 1950s and 1960s, the coup of 1967 and the military junta, which retained government until 1974. Despite significant attempts at progress in recent decades, the economic collapse of 2010 illustrates that Greece still does not have any meaningful economic or governance structure. The current anarchy, though, should not be seen simply as an inability to construct the systems used by other nations in the European Union. The anarchy simply reflects the journey that Greece has travelled over several centuries. While the West broadened access to government, Greeks were excluded from their government and so did not trust those in power. Most Greeks today still do not have meaningful access to their government. With little access to their government, citizens focus on their own private interests and avoid paying taxes because the government provides little in the way of services in return. Taxes have been, and continue to be, used to pay foreign debts.

In Western nations, the economy has been able to grow as a result of the parallel growth of a uniform and accepted legal framework in which trade can occur. The enhancement of private interests through the economy requires a parallel acceptance of public agreements—not just the uniform adoption of agreements but uniform acceptance of those agreements by citizens.

In periods when growth is possible, it is relatively easy to focus just on the economy and not on the parallel agreements requiring conformity, as most citizens are benefiting from this growth. Growth, though, also requires that there be no environmental limits prohibiting it. Both political and environmental limits to growth appear to have been reached. Globally, we have reached the end of the growth cycle. Greece appears to be amongst the first to enter the new 'dark ages' if, indeed, they have not been living in a dark age since the inception of the modern state nearly 200 years ago.

Western Europe experienced its Dark Ages as a consequence of the prosperity of the Byzantine Empire; now Eastern Europe and others are experiencing their 'Dark Ages' while the West prospers. It appears we are now in the midst of another global shift in prosperity as wealth shifts to Asia. The market is a competition. Its aim is to win, for the exclusive use of a few, assets and property to which, at other times in human history, everyone may have had access. In a world of fixed resources, economic growth occurs only at the expense of others.

The market is the means by which we exclude others from the public assets of the 'whole'.

§

It is incongruous that we decide to gather together in a place, acknowledging the benefits of co-operation, and then proceed to make laws that demarcate and protect our private rights to the inevitable detriment of our collective good.

Our society is organised, and our cities configured, according to our perceived duty to established, institutionalised laws and structures. These structures aim to enhance the private interests of the few who are included, at the expense of others.

A just society is one that strives towards moderation, a middle way between excess and deprivation. To avoid these extremes, the principal purpose of government should be the stewardship of nature—that is, to enhance the capacity of nature to support a large collection of people in the one location for the benefit of all. That is, managing the water cycle, the food cycle, the energy cycle and the materials cycle so that the cost of living to a society as a whole is reduced and there is time for personal and spiritual growth. This can only occur on a city-by-city basis. National and international corporate and government structures only shift the focus to trade between cities and therefore away from the city itself, let alone the citizens.

It is not inevitable that the next stage after globalisation is a collapse into a new 'dark ages' before another 'renaissance' of the *polis*. Two thousand years ago, the all-embracing Roman economy allowed the spreading of ideas via the highways and trade routes. One of these ideas was the 'good news' that if you focus on your community, collaborate and share, then a new age of plenty is possible.

This plenty will not come by simply taking from others but, rather, by increasing the capacity of the earth and sharing its wealth. It is possible to transform our societies because it has been done before; when the Roman Empire was transformed from within by collaborative local communities that would later be referred to as Christians. In the next chapter, 'Transparency, Democracy, Liberty' I will explore how the sharing of ideas, transparency and authenticity can transform a society.

Democracy and liberty, the steps that follow transparency, will also be discussed, to illustrate that the sharing of ideas is of no consequence if there is no action in response to them. Justice is therefore not simply an abstract concept of a middle way but also the concrete process of achieving this.

In a City in which everyone has an opinion, conflict is inevitable. According to the pre-Socratic philosopher Heraclitus of Ephesus, both conflict and perpetual change were inevitable. A just city must therefore expect its citizens to participate, to debate and to resolve differences. Justice requires effort. Justice requires courage. "Justice," he said, "is strife."

9

TRANSPARENCY DEMOCRACY LIBERTY

The instruction we find in books is like fire. We fetch it from our neighbours, kindle it at home, communicate it to others, and it becomes the property of all.

~Voltaire

In the previous chapter, I referred briefly to the rational debates of the period prior to the French Revolution in which people asked: 'Why can't we govern ourselves'? One of the principal proponents of these ideas was François-Marie Arouet, better known as Voltaire.

Voltaire believed that ideas could transform the world. That one could help people change the way they function in the world by clearly articulating an alternative then spreading the message as widely as possible. He believed that rather than submitting to the arbitrary rule of King and Church, people could use reason and common sense to govern themselves. In other words, rather than submitting to their fate, people ought to pursue their destiny.

The only problem with spreading such messages is that for much of human history the Kings, Church, and other established authorities, have controlled all the means of communication. Opportunities present themselves, though, when a new means of communication becomes readily accessible.

The advent of the printing press in the fifteenth century allowed any person to share information and ideas without reference to established authorities. It just needed the right person to come along. In 1517, Luther published his ninety-five theses and triggered the Protestant Reformation. It wasn't until 1718, when Arouet adopted the pen name Voltaire, that a strong advocate for social reform effectively used the printing press. He wrote some 2,000 books and pamphlets and 20,000 letters, including arguing for the separation of church and state, freedom of religion and freedom of expression. He was a leading figure of the Enlightenment, and his ideas fuelled the French Revolution and the birth of the Age of Reason, on which our Western societies are based.

Today, the internet offers similar opportunities for reform and it has arrived at an interesting point in human history. The last time we experienced a similar empire so focused on global trade was about 2,000 years ago, when the Rome was at its peak. Not unlike the information superhighways, Roman highways linked all the then known world. Guarded by Roman soldiers to facilitate trade, the roads became a new means of communication and allowed ideas to travel freely.

The Christian Revolution resulted from the spreading of the idea that if you shared your assets and you emphasised personal and community development rather than economic growth, you would no longer need to rely on the all encompassing Roman economy.

The world-wide-web, though, as the name suggests, is far more extensive than the printing press or the Roman highways. Whereas a book or a road connects any one person to many others, the internet can potentially connect every person with every person, or group, immediately, in real time. It is a political gathering place and a market. It has the same qualities as a town square.

Given that the reason we first gathered in cities was for political organisation and for trade and that the internet can provide the same functions, I believe that there can be no question that the internet will significantly alter the way in which we build our cities. Is it possible that future Cities will be governed on line as social or, rather, 'public' networks?

§

Transparency: allowing the light to shine through

"You have one identity", says Facebook founder Mark Zuckerberg, and it is no accident that Facebook is designed that way. According to David Kirkpatrick's *The Facebook Effect*, Zuckerberg argues that, "the level of transparency the world has now won't support having two identities for a single person". In other words "even if you want to segregate your personal from your professional information, you won't be able to, as information about you proliferates on the Internet…."

As the tension grows between what should remain private and what must be made public, we are confronted with the stark reality that one of the fundamental principles upon which Western society rests is the protection of private rights. For example, the protection of private *property* rights forms the basis of all property law. The certainty that flows from that protection provides stability in asset values, which then forms the basis of our economic systems.

Hand-in-hand with the protection of privacy comes the protection of secrets. We now refer to 'private intellectual property' and the protection of 'commercial-in-confidence' information, or 'trade secrets', which are fundamental to most service-based industries. As has also been highlighted by the 'WikiLeaks saga', much of government power is created through the restriction of public access to information, either directly or through the creation of complex bureaucracies. Much of our daily life is also restricted by its very complexity, forcing us to pay for special expertise, secret knowledge, whether it is to access justice, health, education or any other activity. The Western system of social organisation is essentially based on privacy and secrecy or, more accurately, the protection of the private domain.

According to John Ralston Saul, "Everything in the West is secret unless there is a conscious decision to the contrary." In his book, *Voltaire's Bastards: The Dictatorship of Reason in the West*, Western Society, which was originally based on reasonable or rational thought, has left us with the conviction that "truth is a compendium of facts". These facts, in any given area of human endeavour are constructed into the various institutions of knowledge such as law, medicine, technology, even each of the religions. Each institution requires special expertise, including knowledge of special language or jargon, to navigate it. We have been convinced that only these experts can fully understand their part of the system. The manipulator Machiavelli advocated the importance of keeping secrets. He suggested that there is much to conceal if a man wishes to better his rivals.

As a result, the construction of a complex professional persona by all individuals who wish to better their rivals—a public image that is different from our private one—has become a necessary part of the construction of our society. Much of our society is therefore built on the basis of withholding knowledge or information, generally for the purpose of enhancing our economic or other private interests. Ours is a society wherein each person tries to better his rivals—a society of competition. The market is a competition, our workplaces are a competition, our judicial and political systems are a competition.

I have continually argued that we build our cities in accordance with our ideas, after our own image. The creation of two separate identities results in cities of the same form. We create two spatially separate lives—a professional life and a personal life. Both lives have a physical place that needs to be maintained, a set of relationships that must be managed, and daily routine activities that need to be carried out. Rather than assisting us, this separation significantly complicates our lives, and much of the conflict we experience stems from the tension between work and home, or from the need to protect our home from the public realm. The spatial separation also requires that we travel between the two lives, which not only eats away at our time but creates the need for transportation infrastructure of a much larger scale than would otherwise be necessary. Our cities are constructed primarily to manage our fundamental demand that we must have a private life and a public life.

If we continue to press for greater transparency, more public access, to the point where we have only one identity, a single fully publicly accessible identity, then we will be eliminating the conflict between public and private because there will be no private domain. This greater transparency is equivalent to authenticity. We will be one unique person rather than divided and duplicitous.

To better understand the societal consequences of a collapsing private domain, I would like to explore further the reasons why we have constructed a private domain as the basis of our society. To do this, I would like to ask you what your identity is, and what it means to have only one identity—a fully publicly accessible 'facebook' identity.

Is your facebook identity actually you? Isn't this just another compendium of facts—a collection of images and words? Are your comments and your photos actually you? Do they illustrate the full three-dimensional you, in all your depth, in all your colour, in all your moods? Perhaps Facebook provides a comprehensive illustration of various aspects of you, perhaps more comprehensive and more immediate than any other tool in any medium ever available at any time in human history, but it is still not *you*. Your facebook identity is a construction of you by you. It is the image of you that you want to project to the world, perhaps coloured by the perceptions of your facebook 'friends'.

In the context of a society in which everything is a competition, our unconscious aim is to always show ourselves in the best possible light. We aim to enhance who we are. In the first instance, we hide our flaws. We then slightly exaggerate our talents. Then we might attach ourselves to popular people. We like to feel connected to heroes and celebrities so that we can enlarge our own self-image.

This enhancement of our personal identity is not a new phenomenon. Before Facebook and still today, the most common approach for enhancing our image is through our possessions—the clothes we wear, the car we drive, the house we live in, the investments we own—even the companies or organisations we are a part of. These things that we attach to our selves to enhance our self-image is what we have called our ego, or our private domain.

In contrast to artificially enhancing our identity, to be authentic is to willingly reveal one's true character in the public domain. That is, to be transparent about who we are, what we have to offer and what we need. These are also the foundational principals for democracy, the forum in which a group of individuals with similar interests can gather and, in that gathering, the opportunity for each individual to speak freely and honestly in the knowledge that and others will listen without judgement.

Yet our social systems are designed to protect our egos, our private domains. Not only that, our societies are designed to protect private interests so that individuals can compete. In this environment of competition, we must always be protective of our private interests and hide our true selves, we must be inauthentic. As a result of the inauthenticity and competition, some have a significantly larger private domain than others. In summary, our society is one in which we compete with each other to gain exclusive ownership of the world's assets so as to enhance our own self-image relative to others, so that we can better our rivals.

Are we witnessing a global shift, a shift in which we will enhance our personal identities on Facebook rather than in the physical world, in the private domain of our personal assets? Perhaps. Or perhaps we are just adding another layer to our ego, another way of expressing how we are different from or better than others around us.

§

As well as *potentially* supplanting the material world as the way in which we enhance our individual selves, social networking is also changing the way in which we gather in groups for political purposes. As evidenced since 2010 by the dramatic role of social networking in enabling the Arab Spring, it is no longer possible to control the spread of ideas by simply controlling the physical world. Ideas are spread on the internet, and those that resonate gain a momentum and scale in the virtual environment that is impossible to resist when it mobilises in the real world. There is certainly a shift in the way in which we gather in political groups. So social networking is changing the way we define ourselves, both individually *and* collectively.

The internet also provides a third pressure point against our current dual or duplicated life-style and our present system of social organisation. The internet is also a marketplace. Increasingly, we are witnessing the reality that it is much less expensive to have your professional presence on the internet rather than at a physical location—a shop or an office. Online retailing, direct from the producer to the consumer, is the reality of the future. There will likely be a significant decrease in the work necessary in the intermediate processes—wholesaling, warehousing, distribution and logistics, even retailing. The scale of entire segments of our economic structure may be significantly reduced, together with the need for buildings and those parts of the city that provide for them. We are seeing bookstores closing en masse as people shift to ebooks or buy on line. Office space vacancies are also increasing as people work remotely away from the office.

The very reason for gathering in cities, the purpose of urbanisation, was to provide a location for political gathering and for trade. Both of these activities are now happening more efficiently and effectively on line. The city is being supplanted by the internet. The main advantage that the city still holds is its superior access to the internet, its existing infrastructure and networks and the momentum of history. Provided a small collective can satisfy its basic immediate needs—food, housing, perhaps basic health-care and education—if it has access to the internet, it can be located anywhere. Groups of these collectives can then 'gather' as necessary to satisfy larger collective needs or share less common skills. All the essential benefits of urbanisation are possible without the congestion!

It could be argued that perhaps the internet is a better marketplace and perhaps social networking works to remove unwanted governments, but there is no evidence that stable government can be organised on line. To explore this issue further, perhaps we need to rethink our understanding of democracy.

§

Democracy: allowing all lights to shine

The Greek word, 'δημοκρατία' (pronounced 'demo-kratia'), literally means 'citizen-power', where the word for 'power' also means 'to hold'. True democracy is where the citizens have a hold over the decision-making processes, they hold power—not to forfeit it every few years to the elected few but to actually control their destiny. The obvious issue with this is: how do you maintain order and provide stability if everyone is trying to steer the ship? Greek philosophy, certainly from the time of Plato, is unsupportive of democracy as a system of government for this very reason. In *The Republic*, Plato argues that democracy as a form of government is like a ship where all the crew continually challenge each other to take hold of the tiller, to steer the ship, as if there is a daily vote to decide who will be captain. According to Plato, equal power to all and order in society cannot co-exist. Dismissing this egalitarian model of democracy, he then goes on to advocate for a hierarchical model led by the 'philosopher-king'.

Plato, though, was writing a number of centuries after the slow conversion of participatory democracy into the fabricated idea of democracy by representation. He also believed that the masses are incapable of governing themselves and that governance should be left to the philosophers. Yet no philosopher can know your needs and no philosopher can build your relationship with your neighbours so as to provide for your needs.

It is also true, though, that in large-scale societies, negotiating and providing for the needs of the many has always been a difficult process that, in the past, was better left to a few who managed this for the rest; but a world with the immediacy of the internet is altogether different. Before considering how a shift in governance in this new model would be possible, we should explore how a democracy ought to function.

The reason we use the analogy of a ship when referring to a city is that we start with the assumption that a city must travel in a single direction and that all the citizens must either agree with that direction or, if they are in the minority and don't agree, they must conform to that direction anyway. If the purpose of gathering in a city is to make it grow, make it bigger and more powerful, then we *must* all conform. If our aim is economic growth, then the production processes also demand conformity. We have accepted that the highest purpose of government is to maintain or enhance the prospects of economic growth. Economic growth, though, is the means to an end, it's not the end in itself.

We desire economic growth so that we can enhance our personal welfare. What is personal welfare? In the first instance, it is simply food, housing, health care and education. Who provides these? People do. People with learnt skills.

These basic necessities are not provided by complex systems of government, by large corporations or by remote religious institutions. They are not provided more readily when we construct a fifty-storey skyscraper or when we dam a river or send someone to the moon. As clearly articulated in economic theory, our basic necessities are provided when we can readily match the demand or need with the supplier or provider of a good or service.

What does this require? It simply requires, firstly, a meeting place and, secondly, an exchange mechanism. Whereas historically the town square or *agora* was the meeting place for trading, we now refer to the market as a more general idea, and it can be anywhere. Our town squares today contain less activity than in the past because the markets were shifted to purpose built market places, such as shopping centres and supermarkets. Now these alternative market places are being supplanted by the internet. Purchasers and providers meet most efficiently on the internet.

The second element of a market is the exchange mechanism, which is, of course, money. At least it has been money since the Lydians invented coinage in about 600 BCE and this idea was spread throughout Eurasia by the Achaemenid Persians. Before that, exchange was based on barter and credit, that is, on the mutual trust between community members.

We believe we need money as the exchange mechanism in order to create a common ground, a common playing field. Money is an invented idea, a tool that allows us to ascribe a value to our goods and services relative to other goods and services; but how do we ascribe this relativity?

You will recall our earlier discussion about how we enhance our private domain. We enhance our self-image by first hiding our flaws and then slightly exaggerating our talents. We enhance our assets in the same way—by exaggerating the value of our work and undervaluing the work of others. Sellers always want more than buyers want to pay. We compete with the aim of increasing our personal wealth, so we need to take more than we give. Every part of life then becomes a competition—a competition to see who can take the most and give the least.

What does all this mean? Where is this taking us? Actually, it brings us back to the transparency and authenticity that could be possible with Facebook. (I note here that I refer to Facebook as the archetypal social networking site and am not advocating the specific use of this website; any equivalent social networking site could be used). Suppose we used social networking as an alternative exchange mechanism, an alternative to money. Suppose we were completely transparent. Suppose we were completely honest about our identity, our flaws and our talents.

If we had one completely transparent 'facebook' identity, we would have the courage to say what our flaws were and therefore say what we need. We would also not exaggerate our talents, we would say what we can offer and to whom.

Rather than a 'social' network we would now be constructing a 'public' network. Indeed it would be a network that solves both collective and personal needs. In the same way that individuals might clearly state their flaws and ask for their needs to be satisfied, a 'facebook' group could be formed to satisfy a particular collective need. Rather than remote governments that have no personal stake in the satisfaction of many of our collective needs, a facebook group would be a gathering of the interested parties who are willing to address particular issues.

In this way, we can govern ourselves in a more fluid manner, without the concentration of power in the hands of a few. Power would be spread according to the capacity and needs of those who are participating. The benefits are received by those who ask for them, those who participate.

So you may say that this is all interesting in theory, but how would it work in practice? The fact is that it is already happening. Social networking is already transforming the way our economy works. Variously identified as the 'sharing economy', 'peer economy', 'collaborative economy' and 'collaborative consumption', a host of online sites and networks connect a particular need, whether it is a good or service, with an appropriate provider.

These sites facilitate or enable online swapping, bartering, collaboration, sharing and even project funding to satisfy peoples' private needs. It includes ideas such as crowd funding, car sharing, shared use of office space, couch surfing, kitchen surfing, house swapping and many more. These are recorded and curated at the website www.collaborativeconsumption.com.

One description of the sharing economy, provided in a presentation by Rachel Botsman, a leading advocate of collaborative consumption, is that it is facilitating a shift from 'ownership' to 'access'. Botsman says in her presentation:

> *I don't want stuff; I want the needs or experiences it fulfills. This is fueling a massive shift from where usage trumps possessions … where access is better than ownership.*

The 'shareable' website describes itself as "a non-profit news, action and connection hub for the sharing transformation." The description goes on:

> *What's the sharing transformation? It's a movement of movements emerging from the grassroots up to solve today's biggest challenges, which old, top-down institutions are failing to address.*

Botsman argues that the currency of the new economy is trust because users of these sites leave comments about their experiences with each transaction in relation to the other party. This leaves a reputation trail that can be read by other users. Reputation and trustworthiness thus become the new currency—your credit-worthiness, or what I have called your life-supporting credit. Botsman is also convinced that this new economy is causing fundamental changes in society:

> *A "big shift" from the 20th century, a time defined by hyper-consumption, to a 21st-century age of Collaborative Consumption is under way. The convergence of social technologies, a renewed belief in the importance of community, pressing environmental concerns, and cost consciousness are moving us away from the old top-heavy, centralized, and controlled forms of consumerism toward one of sharing, aggregation, openness, and cooperation.*

"Sharing, aggregation, openness and cooperation" are essential elements of democracy. Openness is the transparency I described above, the willingness to openly state your needs. This is now possible on a website that is specifically designed to allow others to satisfy that need whether through financial transactions or through swapping, sharing and collaboration.

The breadth of possibilities is limited only by people's imaginations, and some sites are designed to get people together to modify public spaces, to guide or drive government policy, to complement or supplement the work of government or to protest against government. These activities sit in what we would currently call the political domain rather than in the economic domain. These types of online actions are recorded and curated at www.spontaneousinterventions.org.

All of these examples illustrate how social networking can be used for public purposes, creating a distinct subset, which we could call 'public networking'. Whereas 'social networking' provides a forum for communication, 'public networking' specifically uses that forum to achieve an outcome. Whereas the ancient Greeks separated the social from the public by diluting the wine in the symposium, we now have separate forums individually designed for each type of need.

This effectively takes money out of the equation. We are now developing democratic forums in which people can state their needs, whether an individual need or a suggestion for a collective need, and others can contribute to its satisfaction.

Democracy, the way we have constructed it, has a single aim: that of economic growth, in the hope that economic growth and the market can satisfy all our individual and collective needs. Yet if we demand that we must all travel the same path, to steer the ship in a single direction, then we are enforcing upon ourselves the need to conform to a particular order, whether it is an order imposed by economic processes or tradition or by established structures, governments, religious authorities or others. This demand for conformity is actually the antithesis of democracy.

Democracy, as it is meant to be, is about individual involvement in the delivery of collective needs. It is about individuals gathering and deliberately and willingly forfeiting some of their private interests for particular or specific collective interests, not being forcibly taxed of our private interests by others in the society, who also force us to forfeit our democratic rights every three or four years.

If we see democracy as the tool that permits free speech, then there must be a forum for that speech that will guarantee that the speaker will be heard, and there must be no restrictions on what is said—that is, the speaker must be free. A democratic forum of this nature would allow us to be honest about our flaws and needs so that the right person can be found to address each of these. This, in turn, allows participants to initiate and also to respond to the needs of others. That is, it allows them to distinguish themselves.

A democratic forum encourages the participants to be honest, open and authentic, whereas our current economic and political systems demand conformity and submission.

This would have been the reason for public confession in the early Christian communities; the church, or *ecclesia*, was a democratic forum that encouraged all its members to say what they needed and allow others in the community to help them or to provide for them. This public acknowledgement that we all have unsatisfied needs but that we all also have something to offer also generates a sense of equality.

Once we stand as equals rather than as un-equals, as is the consequence of our current competitive environment, we can then trust each other. In a non-competitive environment, it will no longer be necessary to build a bigger city. Instead, we can focus our spare capacity, our surplus talents, our spare time, our freedom, on building a better city—a more free, more trusting, more caring environment.

§

Liberty: Enlightenment

The Christian Revolution two thousand years ago was a revolt both against the economic structures of the Roman Empire and against the Pharisees and other established religious institutions that demanded compliance with traditional laws. By living communally, Christians had no need of the Roman economy, and the empire slowly started to decline. By emphasising community development and support for each other, these early Christians had no need for the approval of religious authorities. The original meaning of the phrase "the meek shall inherit the earth" has no connotations of weakness. The meek are those who have abandoned the private domain as a means of enhancing their self-worth; it is those who are authentic and honest, the quietly confident, the enlightened. The phrase calls these people to action.

The success of the Christian Revolution and its broad acceptance by many people of the time gave it political power. The Byzantine Empire and the Holy Roman Empire were the institutionalised forms of a groundswell people's movement—a democratic movement where people and communities helped each other. Its institutionalisation, the creation of structures that demand conformity and prohibit the freedom of individuals, meant that the church had simply become the very thing against which Christians had initially revolted.

When Voltaire and the other authors of the French Revolution cried "Liberty, Equality, Fraternity", they were again seeking liberty from King and Pope, freedom from the established authorities. They argued that through the use of 'Reason' and with basic moral values, we *can* govern ourselves. The broad acceptance of 'Reason' as a means by which we can govern ourselves gave broad political power to those who supported that idea. Its institutionalisation into our current forms of government simply means that it has become the very thing against which Voltaire and his friends had revolted.

As transparency again undermines the established systems, we can see the potential for democracy that the internet and 'public' networks can offer. We can see the opportunities for a new market based on trust, selflessness, honesty and authenticity rather than on selfishness, greed and the enhancement of our interests at the expense of others.

We can also see that transparency can offer democracy, can assist in the removal of authoritarian regimes and structures that deny personal freedoms, but liberty does not automatically flow from this. Liberty requires action. Liberty demands constant attention.

While the internet and social networking can offer a new world order, it is up to us and all future generations to ensure that the internet and the key sites that provide our 'public networks' are freely accessible and not controlled by any individual or small group, as this will only guarantee another cycle of oppression and loss of freedom for the majority.

We are living at a unique point in human history. Although many hope that the current economic crisis will be short-lived and we will soon return to growing economies, the idea of perpetual growth no longer seems plausible in the context of environmental degradation and the acknowledged limits of the capacity of the earth to provide.

With economic and environmental crises peaking at the moment of the 'Virtual Revolution' there is a growing sense that, as Voltaire himself said: "The present is pregnant with the future."

10

FROM INFINITY TO ETERNITY

To-morrow, and to-morrow, and to-morrow, creeps in this petty pace from day to day, to the last syllable of recorded time; and all our yesterdays have lighted fools the way to dusty death.

Out, out, brief candle! Life's but a walking shadow, a poor player that struts and frets his hour upon the stage, and then is heard no more. It is a tale, told by an idiot, full of sound and fury, signifying nothing.

~William Shakespeare, *Macbeth*

In this chapter, I explore more fully the relationship between fate and destiny and its consequences for a City. I have already described fate as your 'allotted share' determined by your birth conditions and destiny as '*change* directed at perfecting yourself before you die'. The pursuit of destiny will therefore result in change, both in ourselves and in those around us. Yet, this personal growth or creative change is not the only type of change. Even in the pursuit of economic growth we cause change. So the question becomes: What *kind* of change do we want?

I have argued previously, by reference to the monarchy-democracy continuum, that there are fundamentally only two options for a society: to strive towards monarchy or towards democracy. Whether or not we believe we are currently a democracy is not particularly relevant. What is most relevant is: In what direction we are driving our City? What kind of change are we creating? What are we going to leave our children? Are we heading towards monarchy, where only one citizen has a voice, or are we heading towards democracy and participation by all?

As there are only two possible directions in which a City can strive, it is possible to design our Cities in only one of two ways. I will refer to these two City designs as the infinity model and the eternity model. The infinity model prioritises competition over cooperation because there will only be one ultimate winner—the king or dictator. Consequently, in this model, citizens strive for material growth in order to have the ability to exercise authority over others. Having a head start over others by having a large share allotted to you at your birth or by receiving a significant inheritance then becomes a great advantage. Citizens willingly submit to the obligations and responsibilities imposed on them and are therefore bound by fate. By contrast, in the eternity model, citizens prioritise cooperation over competition, striving towards personal destiny so as to determine what they can offer in that cooperative arrangement. This attitude fundamentally transforms the dynamics of the society.

In the competitive infinity model, citizens challenge each

other's authority by comparing material wealth, so they want to grow their material wealth relative to that of others. This focus on material or economic growth takes us on a path towards infinity, growth without end, which we intuitively understand is unattainable. We believe in growth at all costs and that our banks and other systems are 'too big to fail'. Failure or collapse or death is unacceptable, and we insist on actions that prevent failure and that protect us from loss or death. One consequence of this denial of death is the economic cycles of boom and bust as we strive ever upwards but never plan for a decline or end. Another, more personal, consequence of this denial is eloquently articulated by Shakespeare, in that each day is no different from any other as our progress takes us no closer to an unachievable goal. As we age, the inevitable realisation of our mortality, arising from the imminence of our natural death, highlights the meaninglessness of such impossible aspirations.

The design of our natural environment includes growth as well as decay and death. For a society to function in harmony with nature, it must mimic nature in that regard. Such a society will, consequently, abandon the pursuit of perpetual economic growth and instead acknowledge that growth and decay are simply two facets of living. A society so designed has the character of the proposed eternity model. It does not abandon growth, which is a fundamental human need. Instead, it broadens growth to include personal growth and also embraces decay and death. It is only by acknowledging our mortality and accepting death that we are able to truly live.

To articulate the concept of death is to automatically conjure fear. Yet embracing death does not necessarily, or only, imply a physical death but can also mean the death of our current identity. In the previous chapter, we described how we often define ourselves and create our identity through our possessions, our homes, our clothes, our cars and the like. The death of our identity relates to the abandonment of our material wealth and also the abandonment of the pursuit of further material wealth. This process of 'letting go' is so liberating and empowering that we naturally begin a search for more things that we can abandon. We abandon ideas that bind us; we speak our unmentionable secrets and admit to our greatest flaws. This act of speaking secrets and admitting flaws allows us to find the assistance we need from others. It allows us to cooperate.

This process also gives us permission to reinvent ourselves. By admitting past failures, we can forgive ourselves. By acknowledging that circumstances around us have changed, we can move on and discover something new. Each discovery then takes us to a new level of personal growth and more closely aligns our now more perfect identity with our destiny.

By letting go of our old selves, we make room for new discoveries, and it is this cycle of death and rebirth that takes us to eternity. It is this kind of death and rebirth that Jesus of Nazareth refers to when he says in John 3:3, "Very truly I tell you, no one can see the kingdom of God unless they are born again." It is a cycle of death and rebirth leading to enlightenment that is not dissimilar to the Hindu, Buddhist and Taoist idea of 'samsara' but within the context of a single lifetime.

§

In 399 BCE, a charge was laid in the 'ecclesia', the congregation of citizens in Athens.

> *Socrates is guilty of not believing in the gods believed in by the state, and of introducing other new divinities. Moreover, he is guilty of corrupting the youth. The penalty proposed is death.*

Some 430 years later, a remarkably similar charge of blasphemy against the established religion and of "perverting the nation" was read in the Sanhedrin of Jerusalem and repeated in the Roman Praetorium. The penalty of death by crucifixion was proposed.

Neither man recorded his views; both reportedly claimed that their life was their 'living word', so suggestions of similarities between their lives could be explored only through the accounts of others. By essentially all of these other accounts, these men were the most courageous, selfless, honest and authentic individuals in their respective societies. The reasons for such violent opposition—opposition that ended with state-sanctioned death sentences—therefore appears quite problematic.

I propose that both men sought to encourage, through their own example, a fundamental transition in society—the transition from the infinity model for Cities to the eternity model.

Infinity means to continue or endure without end. The gods of Homer that were inherited by the Athenians and other Greeks, the Olympian gods, displayed the same characteristics as mortal men. They had human form and were vindictive, jealous, self-serving, quarrelsome and competitive. Although they were more powerful than humans, they were substantially no different in character, except that they were immortal; they endured without end.

Despite this superior power and immortality, this infinite existence, the gods did not govern the world. We have already described how Homer suggested that immortality was actually a disadvantage for the gods as it denied them the opportunity to pursue a destiny. Poseidon was the god of the sea and he would never be anything else. Demeter was the goddess of agriculture and she could never develop her niggling interest in hunting because this was the specialty of Artemis.

So the gods were governed by their fate, their birth conditions. For any thinking person, this must have been troubling. Socrates in particular would have found this unacceptable, and one can imagine his search for other ideas. The accusation against him read, in part:

> Socrates is an evil-doer, and a curious person, who searches into things under the earth and in heaven, and he makes the worse appear the better cause; and he teaches the aforesaid doctrines to others.

If there was something higher or more powerful than the Olympian gods, then this was the authority that should be worshipped. Whatever it was that was outside of, or superior to, the infinite existence of the gods, something beyond space and time, Socrates needed to find it. What was fate and how did it govern the world? Indeed, was it fate that governed the world? If not, what did?

I have already described how this challenge, originally proposed in Homer's *Iliad* and *Odyssey*, had a number of significant effects. Firstly, it undermined the authority of the "gods believed in by the state" and therefore also those who gain their authority through the 'knowledge' of the gods. Secondly, it had the effect of allowing greater emphasis to be placed on observations of the real world and so initiated scientific and philosophical enquiry. Thirdly, it was no longer possible to blame the gods when things went wrong in life; it placed greater responsibility in the hands of men. With this greater responsibility came the possibility to do great deeds and to pursue one's destiny.

Despite this sage advice from both Homer and Socrates to take greater responsibility for our lives, both individually and collectively, we still construct our cities on the assumption that individuals cannot govern themselves. Nevertheless, this advice triggered an important change.

I mentioned that the Greek word for fate, 'μοίρα' (pronounced 'meera') is derived from a word that means 'allotted share'. That word is 'μέρος' (pronounced 'meros'), which is also the root of the Latin 'meritum' and the English word 'merit'. 'Meritum' refers to good works deserving a reward. Between the time of Homer and the rise of Latin, there must have been a shift regarding the perception of what it was that actually determined a person's share in life. Your share was not just what you were allotted at birth but also what you were rewarded as a result of good works.

Through the efforts of Socrates, we see the dawning of the idea that the world is created by our individual and collective actions rather than by the gods or by fate. If 'good works' determine our destiny, then it is possible that the world is governed by collective human activity because, unlike one's fate, these actions are within the control of each individual.

We also know that it was not the efforts of Socrates alone that caused this shift because, more than a century earlier, the philosophers of China, India, Persia and Greece were connected through the highways and associated trade of the Achaemenid Empire. Chinese silks are known to have reached Athens as early as 550 BCE, eighty years before Socrates was born.

Confucius was born in 551 BCE, and he expressed the principle, now well known as the Golden Rule: "Never impose on others that which you would not choose for yourself." Buddha was born in 563 BCE and taught about 'karma'. Karma means 'action' or 'doing'; whatever one does, says or thinks, and its resultant consequences, is karma. This action bears like fruit, that is, whatever you do, think or say will be returned in kind. Good thoughts and actions bear good fruit; that is, they have positive consequences.

It does not matter who is most responsible for the Golden Rule. What matters is that the people that we admire as some of the most important figures in the development of our civilisation, Confucius, Buddha, Socrates and Jesus of Nazareth, all sought to encourage this shift from a society that valued birth rights and the conditions of birth to one that encouraged individual responsibility, action and good works. They all sought a shift from the submission to fate, to the pursuit of destiny. They wished for Cities based *not* on the infinity model but on the eternity model.

So what does it mean to shift from a reliance on 'birth rights' to 'good works'? What is it about birth rights that Socrates regarded as detrimental to society? What are the actions or 'good works' that individuals should carry out?

Let us make the assumption that all people are essentially good and that our intention is always to enhance the welfare of all the citizens in a society.

Consider first a model for society that relies on the transfer of birth rights. In such a society, citizens hope that with each passing generation there will be an improvement in welfare. Parents pass on to their children whatever they have inherited in terms of both material possessions and learning, whether this is much or little, as well as the produce of their own sacrifice and labour. Each generation hopes to add value to the family assets so that, in the fullness of time, our children, or our children's children will live a good life. This is the 'infinity model' as it aspires, and has aspired for countless generations, to achieve perfection in the future or in a next life.

The underlying message in the 'infinity model' is always that labour, hard work and sacrifice will bear fruit and that, in the future, life will be better, if not for us then at least for our children. Through this work and sacrifice, each generation hopes to add to the family assets or inherited birth rights. At the very least, each generation is charged not to disgrace the family name by reducing the value of the family assets. We therefore become very protective of everything associated with our birth rights and become indignant when we don't receive what we believe is 'rightfully' ours.

We are also encouraged by the success of others and, in affluent societies, there is much evidence of this success. Many stories are told of difficult and impoverished beginnings that were transformed through hard work, determination and self sacrifice, taking our fellow citizens to a prosperous new life. Truly that must be the good path. Hard work and self sacrifice, both as an example to our children and also to give them a better start—that is, to provide them with birth rights of greater value than we were given.

There are two important points to make in relation to the society described above. The first is that it aspires towards a good life for all 'in the fulness of time'. We begin by accepting that today some are more prosperous than others, but compared to past generations our welfare has improved so we expect that in the 'fulness of time', we will have created a good world for all. This society assumes progress through time—that is, from generation to generation—and aspires towards perfection in the future. This is the growth path towards infinity. It relies on acceptance by the majority that they will not, in fact, enjoy a good life but that they are responsible for the welfare of future generations. It also relies on a belief that there is a reward for a life of sacrifice that contributes towards that beautiful future world. That reward though, will not be enjoyed in this life.

The second point that needs to be emphasised relates to the high value we must place on our family assets. After all, it is through preserving and enhancing these birth rights that we will provide a good life for our children and for future generations. We appreciate the sacrifice and hard work of our parents and want to act responsibly with regard to their free gifts to us. It is imperative that we do not squander these gifts so, consequently, we become more protective. We guard them from others, who are seen as a competitive threat. We become less aware of the principal aim in this long-term project, which is to enhance the welfare of all, and focus instead on our role in the project—that is, to protect and enhance the family assets. We come to accept that the project won't be completed within our lifetime, so our role in it takes on even greater significance: protect and enhance the family assets. If enhancing these assets is not possible, then the importance of their protection is amplified. Some find it unacceptable to be unable to enhance the family assets. Apparently reasonable justifications are developed for the enhancement of family assets at the expense of the assets of others. It is not the law of the jungle we argue, the consequences are not fatal for others, we just want to ensure that our family achieves prosperity sooner than infinity.

Once we have justified this form of competition and the enhancement of our assets at the expense of others, we have compromised the basic premise and objective of the whole project. Indeed, we have compromised these even if we simply aim to protect our assets from others. We began with the assumption that 'all people are essentially good and that our intention is always to enhance the welfare of all the citizens in a society'. If all people are essentially good, why do we need to protect ourselves from them? If we aim to enhance the welfare of all citizens, why are we competing against others and depriving them of the opportunity to achieve prosperity?

A society that is structured to provide a good life sometime in the future is fundamentally flawed because this ideal future is a figment of our imagination. When the project is bigger than a citizen's individual experiences, they will be able to focus only on their role in the overall project. If a project stretches beyond our lifetime, then we need to be told, and have to accept, our role in it. Our birth rights then define our lot in life.

Let us consider an alternative model for society. Once again we will assume that all people are essentially good and that our intention is always to enhance the welfare of all the citizens in a society.

If our aim is to enhance the welfare of others, each action, each day of each citizen could aim to directly and immediately enhance the welfare of his or her neighbour. If we trust that all people are essentially good, then we can depend on each of them to try to enhance our welfare. There is no need to protect ourselves because we trust all those around us. There is also no need to enhance our own assets because our welfare is being nurtured by our neighbours. The enhancement of our personal welfare is simply a matter of trust. It requires that we trust our neighbours to give to us in the same manner as we have given to them. It relies on the Golden Rule.

In the infinity model, the current model by which our societies are structured, we believe that we are good and honest but that no one else can be trusted; we believe we cannot depend on anyone else. Yet this model demands that we trust several vague and nonsensical concepts. We must trust that every person both present and future is equally committed to the same goal. We must trust that this process of asset growth will take us to a society where all will be prosperous. We must trust the advice that our life of work and sacrifice will be rewarded in a next life. We must trust that a society based on competition will eventually result in everyone winning and becoming prosperous. Essentially, we trust these imaginary concepts because we do not have the courage to trust our neighbours.

Our society, based as it is on 'birth rights', relies on loyalty to parents and children above all others. This ensures that each generation is dependent on the one before. We create an artificial sense of security by tying others to us. We build other structures, such as nation-states, corporations and religious institutions that will last beyond our lifetime. We attempt to invest in them the qualities that we would like to endure for the benefit of our children. We trust in the abstract structures because they existed before we were born and we believe they will continue after we are gone. We trust that they will carry our dream into the future.

Yet in this book I have described the countless empires, each of which believed themselves the greatest the world has seen but none of which survives today. Some day, perhaps, we will learn from our own history.

By contrast, a society based on 'good works', or the gifts that we give rather than those we receive, relies on loyalty to our immediate neighbours above all others. Our neighbours are the people with whom we share our daily lives, our daily bread. This may indeed be our family but should not be limited to family. Where family members do not share our daily bread, they are not our neighbours. This does not mean that we cease to love them but that our loyalty and priority is to our neighbours. This is what builds a circle of trust within the community, and this approach was also advocated by Jesus of Nazareth when he said, as quoted in Matthew 10:37: "He who loves father or mother more than me is not worthy of me. And he who loves son or daughter more than me is not worthy of me."

The shift from infinity to eternity is identical to the shift from childhood to adulthood. A child lives according to instruction; a child must initially be obedient and so, essentially, a child's behaviour is a series of re-actions. An adult, by contrast, must act. An adult must initiate and, to initiate, one cannot rely on the instructions of others. The transition from childhood to adulthood is defined by the shift from a reliance on authority to a reliance on oneself, supported by neighbours. It is the shift of attitude away from obedience and towards community.

Both model societies reflect our desire to be part of something bigger than ourselves that will last beyond our deaths, something that will carry hope into the future, something that will, in some sense, make us immortal.

The infinity model carries this hope for our children through the common structures and institutions we create. Although our hopes are *for* our children we prefer to ensure that the direction of their society continues in the way we have determined is best for them through the structures and institutions we have created.

Yet it is rare that institutions themselves become objects of our admiration. Usually, it is the human stories, the contributions and gifts of individuals that we most admire. We look to individuals who have distinguished themselves, usually by giving selflessly to others or to society as a whole; we look to those who have imagined and created something new that benefits others, or to those who have given more than would have been expected. We look to these individuals for inspiration and guidance when we question how to live a good life.

We prefer to rely on institutions but admire human stories. We work tirelessly to maintain our established institutions but usually detest them.

> *Do not lay up for yourselves treasures on earth ... For where your treasure is, there your heart will be also ... No one can serve two masters; for either he will hate the one and love the other, or he will be loyal to the one and despise the other...*
> ~Matthew 6:19-24

By building up our institutions, we leave no time to build human stories. Our institutions fill our lives with meaningless functions and leave us no time to give to others. We protect and enhance our assets and so place our hearts there also; it is not then possible to put our hearts into developing our own stories. We do not learn who we are and how we can contribute to the greater good, the wellbeing of others. We do not learn how we can distinguish ourselves. By expecting that individuals must be indebted for twenty or thirty years, simply for the privilege of being housed, we prohibit the opportunity for giving during that period. This infinity model requires that we satisfy all our inherited obligations and responsibilities before we are entitled to give to others.

By contrast, the eternity model simply places giving to others as the principal concern of each individual. It asks each individual: Who are you and how will you distinguish yourself? How will you contribute to the good of others and the community? What karma do you offer society? This model carries hope forward for our children by trusting them and directly assisting each to learn and grow and to distinguish themselves. It is all about the building of human stories.

Humans differ from other animals because each human life also has a unique human story. Unlike other animals, we do not exist simply as a member of a species but we attribute meaning to our lives and we learn and develop through our experiences. We need, fundamentally, to grow. If we are not growing our spiritual wealth, we are growing our material wealth. In fact, the evidence of spiritual poverty lies in the extent of our material wealth.

This is not an argument for a return to a basic subsistence, communal lifestyle—quite the contrary. The knowledge we have gained in so many areas of human endeavour—medicine, technology, engineering and the like—do not just disappear because of a change in social structure. It is simply a shift in emphasis or priority and begins to create a real 'social value' for other areas of human learning that focus on the human person, including philosophy, spirituality, language, dance, meditation and other traditional knowledge related to personal awareness of the human body and harmony in human relationships. This encourages a shift away from our current exclusive focus on 'economic values' and towards a better balance between social and economic values.

§

The transition from the infinity model to the eternity model can be quite simple. It simply requires those with more material assets than they need to share their surplus with others. The reason for sharing your assets is to reduce the burden of maintaining them. If the person you share these assets with is able to benefit from them, while also assisting in maintaining them, then both parties benefit.

The difficulty with 'giving' lies only in our perception of it. It is perceived as a process whereby one party, the one with excessive material possessions, is the 'giver' and the other the 'receiver'. It creates a hierarchy in which the materially wealthy are regarded as superior. The fact is that both are 'givers' and both are 'receivers'. We currently offer material assets in exchange for money, often in the form of an ongoing debt. The debtor is tied to the creditor and is also responsible for maintaining and protecting the subject assets. If we valued the gifts of time and energy required to maintain assets, then those who offered these would be regarded as equals to those who offered material assets. All relationships should start and end with the regard for our neighbours as equals.

To give up or share our possessions, which have become so tightly connected to our sense of self and family, represents for most not just a loss of identity but a form of death. Yet this apparent loss is more than compensated by the assistance received from others who relieve us of some responsibilities and obligations. This in turn gives us more free time; it liberates us. Cooperation so as to relieve each other of our burdens is the path to freedom from work.

Indeed, through this liberation from work and fresh new human interactions we feel revitalised or reborn. Once a rebirth has been experienced we start searching for other possessions, obligations, responsibilities and aspects of ourselves that we can let go simply to feel that rebirth again or to a greater extent. This death and rebirth is the path to enlightenment.

Liberty from work creates the freedom to write our own story. Yet liberty alone is not sufficient. The way we achieve this liberty, by shifting from competition to cooperation, is equally or more important. This is because the process of cooperating also builds human bonds and so writes more human stories. Work becomes a joy, and so work as we often experience it today—work that is a kind of servitude—is eliminated.

As a consequence, we are free from the servitude of work even when we are working. We are writing our story when we are with others and when we are alone, during work time and during pleasure.

It is not difficult to understand why freedom from work would be offensive to established authorities, as would the suggestion that individuals should shift their focus away from church and state and corporations and focus instead on our neighbours.

Every human story starts at zero. In stark contrast to the economic growth story that takes us from zero onto a singular, linear and monotonous path to infinity, the human story must return to zero. This is the circle of life. Eternity is the journey from zero, through infinite possibilities, passing often close to zero and ending at zero.

> [A]nd I shall repeat the same words to everyone whom I meet, young and old, citizen and alien, but especially to the citizens, inasmuch as they are my brethren ... For I do nothing but go about persuading you all, old and young alike, not to take thought for your persons and your properties, but first and chiefly to care about the greatest improvement of the soul. I tell you that virtue is not given by money, but that from virtue comes money and every other good of man, public as well as private. This is my teaching and if this is the doctrine which corrupts the youth, I am a mischievous person.
>
> ~Plato, *The Apology of Socrates*

This pursuit of virtue advocated by Socrates is the pursuit of your perfect self; it is the pursuit of destiny.

Every human story is different. It starts and ends at zero, but the possibilities between these points are endless, and each journey is unique. Both Socrates and Jesus of Nazareth led unique lives. They were willing to die not only because they were unwilling to deviate from their own unique paths but also because they wanted to highlight the importance of having the courage to pursue destiny.

This is why they have become greater than the immortal Olympian gods. Their spirits live on beyond their physical deaths because the spirit is the part of you that you can create. It is the part of you that is outside your physical body, the collection of things that you have created and have given freely during your life, your good works, the things you have left behind, the things that you leave aside, or outside of you. The free gifts you have given to others.

Never take more than you give; this is the circle of life. Give in the same measure as you have taken and you will be as one with the earth, the same as all the plants and animals but give endlessly and you will elevate yourself above the earth, you will create an immortal spirit.

11

THE THEORY OF EVERYTHING

imaeus is Plato's 'Theory of Everything'. In this, one of his later works, he explores everything from the building blocks of the physical universe to the construction of cities and the nature of God. Through this work we will see how Plato and those who supported or interpreted some of his ideas were able to undo much of the good works of Socrates and, later, of Jesus of Nazareth.

Whereas Socrates placed responsibility in the hands of each individual, his pupil Plato believed that only the philosophers were wise enough to govern and so, in an ideal city, should be given all the responsibility. In *The Republic*, which immediately preceded *Timaeus,* he outlines, for example, how the guardians, or policemen, should have a temperament both compassionate and philosophical yet fierce towards enemies, while the Chief Magistrates should arrange the marriage nuptials to ensure good breeding. These and other elements of his theory lead to the logical conclusion, or more probably stem from the idea, that the capacity to lead exists only in those with the greatest wealth and highest rank, who are also trained in music, gymnastics and philosophy. A city, Plato argues, composed as it is of citizens of different education and capacity, should therefore be governed only by the best, by the philosopher-kings.

This hierarchical world described by Plato is essentially the way we imagine the world naturally *is*—that in any society, some must necessarily have authority over others. Yet policemen and magistrates are inventions that simply align with and support the authority of those who claim superiority, whether through their wealth or their philosophy. The hierarchical model is simply the infinity model described in the previous chapter. In such a model, we need to trust those in authority.

So, isn't this just a way of organising the city? What is wrong with organisation? The problem is not organisation but the assumptions on which it is based. The philosophical basis of Plato's ideas is that the natural world can be understood as hierarchical. That is, everything can be ranked from the best to the worst, or from the most perfect to the least perfect. This is how he justifies his belief that cities should be governed by philosopher-kings, and this is the common thread through all his reasoning.

Thus we have finished the discussion of the universe, which, according to our original intention, has now been brought down to the creation of man. Completeness seems to require that something should be briefly said about other animals: first of women, who are probably degenerate and cowardly men...

The race of wild animals were men who had no philosophy, and never looked up to heaven ... Naturally they turned to their kindred earth and put their forelegs to the ground ... the most senseless of all have no limbs and trail their whole body along the ground.

-Plato, *Timaeus*

Timaeus establishes the 'logical' hierarchy, which has the perfect creator god at the top, the philosopher-king next, the educated man, then the uneducated man, then woman, then various animal species and, finally, the snake at the bottom. In such a conception of the world, it is not possible to perceive nature as an inter-connected and inter-dependent ecosystem, while it also becomes acceptable to discriminate against women and others whom we can readily or rationally rank as inferior to us. Plato designs his ideal city based on his limited understanding of the world around him. Is this our perception of the world?

Plato arrives at his hierarchical world construct by recognising that the world is always changing and that that change is partly a result of our pursuit of growth and of excellence. This perpetual change, together with our differing birth conditions, mean that we are all different. Thus far I would agree. It is the next step in his reasoning that is not acceptable: the belief that these differences determine our status in a hierarchical world. Essentially, Plato is arguing that fate *should* govern the world.

Part of Plato's justification stems from his love of 'reason'. As the great advocate of reason, Plato assumes that rational thought is perfection.

> *That which is apprehended by intelligence and reason is always in the same state; but that which is conceived by opinion with the help of sensation and without reason is always in a process of becoming and perishing and never really is.*
>
> ~Plato, *Timaeus*

He argues that 'opinion' is inferior to 'reason' because opinion is uncertain, while reason provides certainty and permanence. Opinion, like theory, is always in a state of change until a matter is finally settled, at which point we arrive at the truth. Therefore, he argues, everything that is changing is aspiring towards something, towards an absolute, an ideal, a supreme truth. As the world is always changing, it must, therefore, be aspiring towards a perfect ideal, a perfect world. This place (not, of course, a physical place) must be outside the created universe because the universe is always changing. This 'place' where everything has reached perfection, is where Plato's creator god exists.

So our ideas about the 'nature' of the Creator and of heaven as a place of perfection stem from Plato's construction of reality, as later canonised into a supreme truth by the Christian church. This makes our world a place of imperfection and its occupants perpetually imperfect (that is, sinful) until they depart for the perfect world. As a result, heaven and earth are opposites that never meet, separated by a chasm that cannot be crossed.

We also align linear, rational thought with perfection, so everything that is not rational is irrational, and by this we mean flawed and imperfect. Yet intuitive or lateral thinking is not rational. When attempting to find the truth, it is important to be able to link across ideas and disciplines, across different rational lines of thought. This allows us to go beyond a rational line of reasoning to a connected flow of ideas.

This rational approach, where the opposite of a positive trait is necessarily negative, is all pervasive in Western society, and we quickly identify everything as good or evil and rarely acknowledge that both of these opposites can be found in everything. For example, to be 'responsible' is a positive trait but the negative trait 'irresponsible' is not its only opposite. The opposite of responsible is also 'free of responsibility'. We perpetually demand loyalty, requiring that others must satisfy their obligations and responsibilities and, consequently, we preclude freedom. We preclude freedom simply because we cannot perceive opposites as complementary, as two halves of a whole. Is it necessary for everyone to perpetually 'be' responsible? Is it not possible to imagine that we should 'act' responsibly and then be allowed to be free.

In the next chapter, 'The Ecstasy of Yang', I will explore this duality and the complementarity of opposites more fully.

Plato's construction of reality has also locked us into a particular perception of truth. Truth, according to Plato, can be discovered by exploring many theories or opinions and subjecting them to rigorous testing. The testing weeds out those opinions that are false until you are left with the 'correct opinion', which is deemed then to be the truth. This is the scientific approach and has been extremely useful when applied to matters that can be observed and tested.

The word 'orthodox' is derived from the Greek for 'correct opinion'. When applied to untestable ideas, this approach can lead to the enforcement of one opinion over another. Such claims regarding the 'orthodox' truth about God and the 'correct' way of living stem from Plato's hierarchical construction of reality but are nothing more than opinion enforced as law.

Numerous 'orthodoxies'—opinions that are enforced as truths—are fundamental to Western thinking. The orthodoxy that economic growth is the ultimate good and therefore the principal purpose of all governments is an important example. It is an orthodoxy that creates a hierarchy in our society. The hierarchy is then used to justify the orthodoxy.

Economic growth aligns well with the orthodoxy that heaven is inaccessible and that we are always imperfect. In an environment where we can never access or understand heaven, our natural striving towards excellence can readily be steered in any direction by those who cast themselves as superior— the philosopher-kings who desire to be called Your Excellency, Your Honour, Your Majesty, Your Eminence. In the economic domain, the majority are steered towards maximising material wealth, which only enhances the 'perfection' of the wealthy. In the spiritual domain, the majority are steered towards an appreciation of their own sinfulness, their inadequacy, and their inferiority by comparison to the orthodox ideal, which again enhances the authority of the philosopher-kings.

We aspire, not knowing what we aspire towards. We feel inadequate and imperfect because perfection apparently does not exist in this world. The only available ideas of perfection are those of material wealth and authority over others. In such a hierarchical world, many compete for the few offices of authority or for a larger share of the limited wealth of the earth, imagining that these represent a striving towards heaven. When heaven is available for only a few, life becomes a competition and a competitive environment encourages aggression.

§

I'm now going to take you off on a little tangent to describe how aggression creates and reinforces our social structure.

In the late 1950s a most unusual experiment began to be conducted in Siberia. A group of 130 silver foxes were collected from fur farms and taken to a nearby genetics institute. Genetics was in its infancy, but biologists Dmitry and Nikolay Belyaev wanted to understand the relationship between domesticated dogs and wolves. They believed that the differences were at a molecular level but the beginnings of modern DNA sequencing were still two decades away.

They decided to recreate the evolution of wolves into dogs by starting with wild silver foxes. Each generation of fox kits were tested for their reaction to human contact, and the most approachable were selected to breed for the next generation. Within a few years, they were producing foxes that were not just unafraid of humans but were actively seeking to bond with them. Soon, the physical appearance of the foxes also started to change. After just nine generations, some foxes had floppy ears, some had spots on their coats, and others had curly tails, which they started to wag. They also started to whine, developing a language to communicate with humans.

Essentially, they began to express their individuality and reach out for ways of connecting with their new clan. Once the demand for conformity, as imposed by the alpha male, was removed, each individual was free to express its own individuality.

The consequence of a competitive environment is that the most aggressive find their way to the top. Aggressive does not necessarily mean violent. The most aggressive are those who are most insistent on a particular orthodoxy. They impose their way of thinking and behaving on others. They preclude individuality and demand conformity. They describe the flaws of others as imperfections that, when modified in accordance with their orthodoxy, will become more perfect.

We must begin to see our flaws not as imperfections or inadequacies but as opportunities. When we accept and acknowledge our flaws, we can accept the assistance of others. Similarly, when we acknowledge our talents, we know what we can offer others. It is our differences that allow us to complement and cooperate with others—our immediate neighbours in our new clan.

The reason we should aim to complement and co-operate with neighbours is that finding our place within a small group is a step towards finding our place in the world and also a step towards appreciating our inter-relationship with our natural environment. To explore these communal and natural inter-relationships requires an understanding of the physical world and a recognition of how our ideas about the physical world have changed since the time of Plato.

§

In *Timaeus*, having described the supernatural world and the natural world at the human scale, Plato turns his mind to understanding the construction of the physical world.

> *In the first place, then, as is evident to all, fire and earth and water and air are bodies. And every sort of body possesses solidity, and every solid must necessarily be contained in planes; and every plane rectilinear figure is composed of triangles...*

So begins Plato's construction of the world as a combination of fundamental shapes. These shapes are known as the Platonic solids, which are all composed of triangles. They are described as the perfect solids, the perfect forms, which combine to create firstly fire, earth, water and air then, from these, all of the physical world. Given that these ideas were expressed many centuries before a thorough understanding of atoms and compounds, the idea that everything was a composition of fundamental units that were combined in an ordered way was well ahead of its time.

Yet even though everything is composed of atoms and ordered compounds, very little of our physical world, as we experience it, can be described simply through the relationship of atoms and compounds. Some crystals look like magnified versions of their basic compound structure but most of the world appears disorderly rather than orderly.

The disorder is best described through Chaos Theory and in particular the idea of fractals. Fractals are composed of a real number and an imaginary number, formed into an equation that is repeated over and over again. Fractals are used in computer animation to create a very real-looking imaginary world. The best mathematical way to describe our world is through fractals, a merger of the real and the imaginary combined into a formula and repeated over and over again.

The repetitions that occur over and over are the rhythms of nature. Those rhythms create our climate, which dictates the movement of water and wind, which in turn create our natural landscape. The natural landscape together with the climate create certain environmental conditions, another rhythm, that allow life to develop. Out of these rhythms comes life in the form of DNA, which is a formula that can be repeated over and over to create a life form.

The relationship between all these rhythms, the rhythms of life, is the flow between the real and the imaginary, the union of the real and the imaginary to create a whole. The real is the material object itself, whether animate or inanimate—its own structure, its crystalline form, the combination of compounds from which it is formed. The imaginary are all the outside forces that act on the object. Nothing in our physical environment exists on its own. Everything exists as a relationship to the environment around it. It is only through an understanding of the forces outside of yourself that you can understand yourself. Life is a balance between the real and the imaginary, the self and the other. More than this, the real self and the imaginary self are opposites that form two halves of the whole person.

This idea, that there is something that is not part of our physical bodies, is not tangible but is nevertheless an intrinsic part of who we are, has been expressed in many ways throughout human history.

Through the Christian tradition, we refer to this other part as our soul. Socrates instead referred to his daemon. His daemon was not within him but rather always walked next to him. Philosophers and artists would talk to their daemon as if it were another person. The daemon was the expression of their perfect self and the embodiment of truth. Truth, they believed, was just there, next to them. They just needed to wrestle with their daemon, to wrestle with the truth in order for it to be revealed. Truth, they believed, could not originate *from* an imperfect person but rather it was revealed *through* them, flowing through them from an outside source.

The Romans referred to the 'genius', that is, the divine nature present with every individual. Artists would consult their genius for inspiration and also blame it when that inspiration was not forthcoming. Artists took neither credit nor blame for their work, their art was transmitted through them from the gods.

The 'jinn' or 'genie' of Arab folklore, are supernatural creatures that live in a parallel world. One type of jinn is the 'qarin', which means 'constant companion'. The 'qarin' apparently push people to do evil things and to disobey Allah, but it is unclear whether this aspect of their character has been demonised in the same way as the Greek daemon.

This conversation with an imaginary 'person'—the daemon, genius, or qarin—is a way of speaking honestly to yourself and listening to your heart. Yet it also allows us to connect with something greater, to feel less alone and to be part of something more meaningful. It is fundamentally the same as prayer. Through a sincere conversation with the source of truth, who is always there next to us, our own truth will be revealed.

§

Approximately 2,500 years ago, an extraordinary shift occurred on the Eurasian continents. Confucius, Buddha and Socrates added an additional element to this 'conversation' with the Source of Truth. They insisted that this was the guiding principle behind a life well lived. To live well was to actively pursue the truth, not just with your daemon but with anyone who was willing to participate in a dialogue. To be fully alive necessarily required embracing others, and the *dialogue* took on great significance. To realise one's full potential was not just an internal and individual journey but a communal journey. The 'imaginary other', the part of our self that was not part of our physical body had now taken on the form of the people around us. The objective was to pursue virtue or personal enlightenment, but now others, both imaginary and real, could and should assist in this. In effect, truth had become incarnate, it had taken the bodily form of our neighbours.

Some five centuries years later, Jesus of Nazareth took the pursuit of truth to yet another level. He believed that neighbours were so important to the pursuit of truth that our principal focus should be on *their* growth and development and that our own personal development would be a consequence of our focus on, and care for, others. He also believed that we should be more conscious in choosing the people we gather around us, that we should form communities in which everyone shared their talents and sought assistance where necessary. In this way we could satisfy both our physical and spiritual needs more effectively. This required that all the members of the community gather regularly (in communion) to openly and honestly discuss their needs and offer their talents. The creation of a forum for collaboration and dialogue was the reason for the gathering of the ecclesia and for public confession in those early communities.

§

In the continents not influenced by these Eurasian ideas, a far older understanding of how we should describe our 'larger selves' remained. For example, Aboriginal Australians do not regard themselves as individuals but as part, not only of their community, but also the land on which they live. Their traditional way of life was structured around caring for their land. This 'connection to land', especially that geographical area with which they are ancestrally connected—their 'country'—is difficult for modern city-dwellers to appreciate given our deliberate disconnection from the land.

One analogy that may be useful is to imagine a modern city like a zoo. Early zoos were just a collection of cages but the animals within them soon became lethargic, perhaps depressed and ceased to behave in their usual manner. They were soulless. It became clear that to fully appreciate a wild animal, you either had to travel to its natural environment or reconstruct, as accurately as possible, an imitation of that environment. We now appreciate that it is not possible to protect animal species without protecting their environment. Animals and plants of all species form an interconnected network, where each relies on all others to a greater or lesser degree. We cannot build our cities, protected and separate from the natural environment, we are part of that same ecosystem.

Today, our cities are like gilded cages. They glisten and sparkle and are full of so many wondrous things, but many travel around them unhappy and soul-less; it is as if our daemons have been cut off from us. We have come to accept that only the lucky few have the X-Factor, yet our genius is just there, next to us, waiting to be wrestled with, waiting for us to begin the search for our perfect self, waiting for us to search inside our hearts for the truth about ourselves and to say it aloud—first to our daemon and then to our neighbour. Our genie is waiting to grant us our wishes, waiting for us to ask sincerely and to pursue the Truth.

You are more than just your body. You are part of something greater—your community and your land. Listen to your daemon. Ask your genius. Do others in your immediate community impose their orthodoxy or is everyone encouraged to find their rhythm, their resonance frequency? Are you free to make a valuable, meaningful contribution or do you feel trapped by routine? Are you regarded as an equal or is there a social hierarchy?

Does your land resonate with you? Is the care of your land a shared common purpose for all the members of the community? Do you feel that you are part of it or are you excluded from parts of it?

Do your land and your community help you to discover the truth about who you are, your perfect self? The pursuit of your 'perfect self', the perfect you, is the pursuit of happiness.

12

THE ECSTASY OF YANG

We have previously described the meaning of ecstasy as stepping outside of your self, or thinking beyond your natural needs. Taking this idea a step farther, to be ecstatic is to think outside the box—that is, to be creative. Further still, we could say that to let go of your natural self is to find your spiritual self. This is why the Greeks believed that your spirit, which they called a daemon, lived next to you, not inside you. Each person consisted of spirit and body walking side-by-side.

The Chinese also theorised that each person, in fact all things, consisted of two complementary personalities, the feminine yin and the masculine yang. The yin was the body, bound to the earth and natural laws, concerned about safety and stability, while the yang was the spirit that was yearning for heaven.

What do ecstasy, daemons, yin and yang have to do with building cities? Again we come to the realisation that our ideas are the foundations of our cities. We construct our world by creating or inventing something new or doing something different, or at least differently. This new creation is then absorbed into our body of knowledge, and our physical world is altered. We create our world through our imagination. Through our yearning for creativity, for art, for music, for new inventions, we are able to step outside the known way of doing things and imagine new and better ways. The imagined ideal is the domain of creativity and spirituality, the domain of ecstasy and of yang.

In this chapter, I will aim to demonstrate how our world, our cities, have been constructed through two competing world views, the second of which arose with advent of agriculture 10,000 years ago. I will argue that the nomadic lifestyle has, since that time, been painted as the wrong way to live and the sedentary agricultural lifestyle is the correct way to live. Our societies have consequently been constructed so as to be concerned about and to favour security, safety, stability and the protection and preservation of our bodies. As a result, our spirits and our creativity are not always allowed to flourish.

To be concerned for your spirit means to stop thinking about your body, to stop worrying about material needs, whether you have *enough* and whether you are safe and secure. To be concerned for your spirit is to be concerned for others outside of you—your community, indeed your neighbour.

Yin and yang, body and spirit, man and daemon show themselves in almost every facet of our daily lives and in every part of our social structure. I hope to illustrate that they are not only equally essential and mutually compatible but are, in fact, complementary opposites. Both are necessary to create a 'whole' person or a 'whole' City.

§

Even before the Agricultural Revolution and before even the domestication of animals by pastoralists, the earliest human communities were hunter-gatherers. The gatherers collected from a sure and steady food supply, while the hunters took greater risks for much richer prizes. Whereas the gatherers stayed close to the protection of the cave, the hunters would venture farther away and explore surrounding territories. Whilst the gatherers maintained and sustained the home, the hunters, and later the explorers, sought growth, new ideas, to explain mysteries, to discover 'better' ways in distant places.

The rewards of the risk-takers were shared with those who preferred or needed safety and security, while the certainty of a secure home and steady food supply were offered freely to the risk-takers. Communities were composed of members with complementary and equally valued characteristics. Both were necessary for the community to function smoothly.

In the West, until just a few decades ago, we routinely equated the home-maker characteristics with women and the risk-taker or growth-seeker characteristics with men, ascribing roles and responsibilities accordingly. These ascribed roles have been a source of tension for both men and women. In the East, the earth-bound 'yin' and the heaven-seeking 'yang' were referred to as feminine and masculine qualities but it was understood that everyone and everything contained both yin and yang energies within them and the force of those energies changed within the same person over time. For example, a young child, whether male or female, is governed by yin-energy, needing support and protection. As the child grows he or she ventures farther and farther from home, building yang energy. We refer to 'rebellious youth', but this is simply a growth phase, a change that should be accommodated and supported so that adults have a balance of both yin and yang energies. Later we may 'settle down' and marry—a return to yin prominence—while in our forties or fifties we may have a mid-life crisis as the yang energies, restrained for many years, begin to dominate again.

It is interesting to note the negativity of the language with which we describe any expression of yang energies, 'rebellious youth' and 'mid-life crisis'. As a property-based society we encourage home ownership and the anchoring of each person to a place and a job; we encourage stability, certainty and permanence. As a consequence, many feel trapped by responsibilities and obligations, which develop into routine, consequently precluding personal growth and development.

Although we may individually support and encourage quests of discovery and the exploration of new ideas, this runs contrary to our social structure, which is formed through establishments and institutions. We are starting to accept the idea of the 'gap-year' after the completion of school, and divorce no longer carries the stigma that it once did, but individuals must still break out of established society—the stable job and home life—in order to search for their heaven.

§

It is considered that a fundamental aspect of the Western perception of the world is that in all things there is a right way and wrong way, that life is a battle between good and evil, that good is discovered by following the right way, and that a failure to follow the established 'right way' leads to evil.

In Chapter 5, 'The Star of David', I referred to the Genesis story in which Adam is forbidden to eat of the fruit of the tree of knowledge of good and evil. I indicated that the meaning of this was that no one should claim to know what is good and what is evil because it cannot be known in any absolute sense. Therefore those who do claim to know it are doing so for their own benefit.

In this chapter, I argue that rather than seeing the world as black and white or right and wrong—that is, two contrasting and mutually exclusive opposites—we should seek the Truth in balance and harmony between complementary opposites. Indeed, yin and yang are not just complementary opposites but, as the symbol illustrates, yin flows into yang and yang flows into yin. Each side has a spot of the opposite character, representing a seed. Yin contains the seed of yang and therefore is able to transform into yang and vice versa. The spiritual rises up out of the material but is not superior to it.

Similarly, through the idea of ecstasy, the Greeks suggested that you step outside your natural state into your daemon so that you can look at yourself objectively, the way others see you; and when in your natural state you should be thinking about how to enhance your spiritual state. They regarded it almost like a dance between your alternate states, or that to live a good life required that you *wrestle with your daemon*. A good life was one that made good use of one's daemon, where the daemon and the man wrestled often and so were equally matched. When a man was equal to his daemon he saw himself in the same way as others saw him, he knew and understood himself. The state was referred to as *'eu-daemonia'*, literally 'good-daemon' or healthy spirit. References in the Christian Bible to 'beatitude' or the state of 'blessedness' are translations of this word. The reference in the American Declaration of Independence to the 'pursuit of happiness' was intended by the philosophers of the time to refer to this same idea.

This was a state of lasting and inner happiness that comes from understanding yourself, both your strengths and your weaknesses. By acknowledging your strengths, you know what you have to offer to others, while knowing your weaknesses allows you to be open to the assistance of others. The free giving and receiving of support allows us to build meaningful and useful bonds with others and is fundamental to the construction of a community.

The pursuit of the discovery of self, to 'know thyself', so as to understand what it is you can offer the world, is the pursuit of happiness and is of course intimately linked with ecstasy.

§

This view of the world as yin and yang, as an earth-bound versus heaven-seeking duality, is expressed in many ways throughout our societies. The most obvious example is the conflict between secular and sacred. We may refer to ours as a secular society, a society grounded in knowledge and facts, but many still pursue religious activities, searching for heaven, a truth that lies beyond the facts.

Another way in which we express this same tension is the relationship between science and religion. Science claims to be grounded in facts, suggesting that a universal truth can be established only through a comprehensive understanding of the physical world. By contrast, religion relies on faith, claiming that the physical world can truly be understood only once you accept and trust a given universal truth. We also have two forms of education. In the arts, we pursue ideas, while in the sciences we try to understand the facts. When designing an object or a building, we wrestle between form and function, between the ideal image and the practical application, between the beautiful appearance and the usability.

This earth-bound versus heaven-seeking duality pervades many aspects of our societies because it is a fundamental aspect of human nature; indeed, that is how our brains are built. To reinforce the point I made earlier that yin and yang energies exist to different degrees in all of us, think of what neuroscience tells us about our brains. Our brains have a left hemisphere and a right hemisphere. Our left brain is detail-driven, logical, analytical and perceives the world verbally, through language, while our right brain is regarded as the centre of creativity, with spatial and global perception, perceiving the world through images. The logical left side is our yin side. Logic requires previous knowledge, each step is based on the step that came before. Our creative right side perceives the world as a whole, as a snapshot, a single image. Whereas our logical left brain is grounded in, and grows out of, our existing knowledge; our creative right brain sees the whole picture, the yang heaven, and interprets the connections that must exist to create the beautiful and unified whole. When our linear and lateral thinking converge, we sense harmony. The sense of peace and beauty that comes with harmony occurs when both sides of our brain give the same answer, when the logical path takes us to a coherent, focused and understandable image of the future, when the language explains the image and the image explains the language. We feel tension when our intuition and logic are telling different stories.

So since this is how our brains work, this duality, our yin and yang natures permeate all aspects of our lives, including the way we construct our societies on a daily basis. The political domain, where we create the laws that determine how we relate to each other, is often a contested environment between conservatives and liberals. While the yin conservatives will claim that the existing systems, the established order as we know and understand it must be conserved and supported, the liberals will advocate an altogether different approach, an imagined ideal. Liberals have perennially argued that the established systems no longer serve a modern world and that they must be abandoned for a better way. The imagined, ideal, or better way reflects our yang nature, our desire to reach heaven, the perfect world here on earth.

We also find that the political environment reflects the struggle between private and public interests; between economic interests on the one hand and social or communal concerns on the other. Although capitalism and socialism are opposing political ideologies, most Western nations now have two entrenched political parties, both located somewhere in the centre of the spectrum. We generally accept that some level of social welfare and public infrastructure are necessary, while we also accept that individuals should be able to satisfy private interests. Both communality and individuality are necessary. Unfortunately, we find this midpoint by compromising both ideals. Our societies are an unstable consensus of dissatisfied individuals with no sense of community. We cannot achieve either communality or individuality if we have to compromise both; we must simply accommodate both types of activities in our lives.

So how do we accommodate both individuality and communality? We need to perceive these as complementary rather than mutually exclusive opposites, so the first step is to create physical spaces in which they can be accommodated.

We have previously described the household and the economy—the private domain—as the environment in which we satisfy our basic needs. We also indicated that the public domain is the time and place for being concerned about others outside of your household. So, in designing a City, the spaces outside the household are just as necessary as the houses, if not more so. We currently expend far too much effort in designing our houses, and city planning is mostly concerned about extending the city by providing for more houses. Too little conscious effort is allocated to the creation of meaningful spaces for collaboration, sharing, creativity, political action and so on. Most often these are left-over spaces or ones otherwise retrofitted into the city.

We therefore accommodate both individuality and communality by actually providing spaces for these activities, in all their forms, to occur within the physical environment of the City.

I have previously argued that in building a City it is important to consciously separate the public and the private domains so that a time and space for freedom from work is regularly available to all. The idea of yin and yang tells us that these are two halves of the whole, that they are complementary opposites, that the one grows out of or transforms into the other. This means that through the conscious creation of a public domain we can more readily satisfy our private needs but that the public domain cannot be created unless we are willing to give up private assets, including private time and privately owned spaces.

It also means that, unlike the Greek solution that created a division between men and women, all citizens should be able to move freely between the private and public domains.

§

We intuitively appreciate the beauty of a public domain because, as a separate and deliberately created time and place, we are not bound by existing systems, we can create something completely new; we can make up the rules. I say this is intuitive because most of us will have done this often. Think of your childhood in the school yard or back yard with a group of friends. You gather together at an agreed time and place, and play a game with a set of rules. These rules are sometimes adopted from existing standards but are usually amended to suit the gathered group. We amend the rules to suit ourselves because we want to start off as equals. We want a fair game because we want to see who will distinguish themselves; who is the 'best and fairest'. The idea of sport generally is to set aside our differences and our inequalities, to set aside our relative wealth or poverty, our national or ethnic or other differences and compete as equals. We define a time and place where we can gather as equals and compete within a new and agreed set of rules to see who stands out, who distinguishes themselves.

When we dance, we again create a public domain. The dance floor is the space and 'while the music plays' is the time. We observe from the side to see who the best dancers are; who distinguishes themselves. We are not looking for technical precision but for beauty and harmony, we are looking for the X-factor—who steps beyond the rules to create a new reality, something more beautiful. We can't define the X-factor because it exists beyond our existing understanding; it is a new creation, but it can be recognised because it carries the quality of harmony. Creativity is possible only in a created environment, a time and place that is outside our existing systems, where we stand as equals and search for the X-factor.

The tango is perhaps the most admired dance because, when danced well, two bodies act with a single mind; and this is the ultimate purpose of creativity, the ultimate expression of our yang desire to find heaven. The heaven is in the discovery of a way to unite our yin and yang energies into a cohesive, singular and perfect whole. Love is the ultimate harmony and, therefore, the ultimate expression of creativity. This unity of mind between two people is only the first step to the creation of a community, which is the unity of mind and harmony between many people.

On a more intimate level, the first requirement in the practice of tantric sex is to set aside a time during which there will be no interruptions. A space is then created that has music and aromas that make it feel different, even other-worldly—again a time and space in which eternity can be discovered and experienced.

While we may admire individual sportsmen, it is team sports that have the broadest appeal. This is because the public domain is the domain of collective interests, we are searching for collective efforts, how a group of individuals can gather to form a unit, a cohesive entity that distinguishes itself.

This, then, is how we build a better city; by building the community first—not just a random collective but a team—a team of complementary players that fit together and are willing to work together. The team must gather regularly at a fixed time and place, and focus not on themselves but on each other, on how to create a team bond, a team spirit. They must look at each other honestly, look for gaps in their skills and abilities and find the right person to provide these. By putting together a team of complementary players, we can satisfy our needs more efficiently and then, with our spare capacity, we can do nothing or satisfy other desires or assist other communities. The aim, though, must be to satisfy our natural needs first and as efficiently as possible so that we can create that spare capacity—the free time, the public domain in which we can create a better world.

§

The suggestion that we should create a fixed time and space for gathering together may appear contrary to the idea of the explorer on a quest of discovery searching for heaven. How is it possible to argue that we should allow or encourage freedom in the city and at the same time argue that we need to create a fixed time and place where we can build a community? Is there a contradiction here?

I would argue that there is no contradiction. Each local community needs its fixed time and space to develop its team spirit. Each individual needs the freedom to travel between communities, within the City's network of local communities, in order to find the place where he or she can make the best contribution.

The argument for freedom is about our ability to leave home and go on a journey of self-discovery, the yang search for heaven. How readily can we disconnect from our responsibilities, obligations, loyalties and attachments? The web of ties—family, job and other routines—all keep us perpetually anchored to the one place and to our fate. How can you find heaven if you can't travel and look for it? How can you experience ecstasy if you are always bound to the same routine? How do you step outside yourself, expand your awareness, if you never do anything differently? More importantly, how can you *choose* a team, a community of complementary players if you can't leave home or work to look for it? It is this freedom to choose something other than the existing situation that allows for the pursuit of destiny and therefore of happiness.

This is what I mean by freedom—the freedom to readily move on to another place whenever our current circumstances are no longer suitable. More generally, it is the freedom to let go of our world as we know it and create something new.

This appeal for greater freedom in the City should not be regarded as a call to abandon our lives as we know them and start on a journey. That would suggest that we value our search for heaven above our earthly needs. The argument is for greater acceptance and encouragement of change. Continual change is perhaps more uncomfortable than permanent stability. This is a dance—a dance between yin and yang, between stability and mobility. As in hunter-gatherer societies, both are essential for a community to function smoothly.

What is the best way of maintaining stability while also allowing freedom?

§

I had sometimes wondered why the apple in the Apple Inc. logo had a bite taken out of it. I thought it might be a subliminal message saying that we should take a bite and eat from the fruit of the biblical tree of knowledge. Then I realised that the Genesis story referred to the *tree of knowledge of good and evil*. I then Googled my question and found that the bite was just intended to ensure that the apple wasn't confused with a cherry. Anyway, I say all this because I wanted to talk about internet and the idea of a tree of knowledge.

I believe that the internet is *our* tree of knowledge. The virtual world is our yang heaven, the complementary opposite of our real world with the ability to connect us and create a connected human consciousness. With our desktop computers, we can travel the world while remaining at home. With a smart phone or a tablet computer we can stay connected to home while travelling the world.

With social networking, we are able to form communities and stay connected wherever we are. The social contracts, the agreements between the members, can now be stored in a shared location on the cloud and can be reviewed at any time. The community can make and amend their own rules at any time. This is true democracy. The freedom to make and amend the rules you live by.

Imagine the world as a network of village communities, each of which guarantees its members and any visitors, food, housing and other basic necessities. This provides the yin stability and safety. Imagine, then, numerous yang individuals or groups travelling from community to community, offering their skills in exchange for food and lodging. These visiting skills would provide whatever is not available in the village or would complement available skills. Some websites such as www.workaway.info, www.HelpX.net and www.wwoof.net are already linking workers with hosts, but they generally need to expand the range of skills they are seeking.

Within each village, the design could provide a yin sanctuary for each citizen, and these would be connected by a range of different collaborative spaces of different types and different scales, for all imaginable purposes. These designs would think about all the private and public activities of the citizens through each day and throughout the year.

Communities would collaborate or gather into larger collectives to satisfy more complex needs or to share rarer skills.

Imagine a world where, instead of anchoring each other to a place, we allow each other to be mobile. Rather than being fixed, we could be free. Imagine also if our 'facebook' status could simply be 'yang', that is 'don't expect any further updates until I'm ready to connect again' or 'Yang' with a capital 'Y', meaning 'I'd like to re-invent myself so my personal history is no longer a guide as to who I am today or will be tomorrow'.

Rather than demanding compromise, we should accept that change is inevitable. Instead of waiting to be frustrated before escaping, we could regularly ask ourselves whether we could be more useful to others rather than to those to whom we are currently connected. By asking ourselves this question we begin to understand and know ourselves and know what we have to offer. Asking yourself: "Who am I and what do I have to offer the world?" is the pursuit of happiness.

Imagine a world where, rather than striving to expand our material wealth, we sought to satisfy our material needs as efficiently as possible so that we could create the spare capacity, the time and space, the public domain, in which we could help others.

Imagine a world where helping others started with providing free access to the whole body of human knowledge, to the fruits of the tree of knowledge. Where learning and education wasn't about being more productive but about being more creative, not about growing our material wealth but our spiritual wealth, or where 'more productive' meant more efficiently satisfying our basic needs and thus producing more spare capacity. Imagine a world where that spare capacity was utilised to create greater harmony between us, or to share knowledge and ideas, or to explore, or simply to stop and wonder at the beauty of the world.

Imagine.

Imagine the ecstasy of yang.

13

THE RHYTHM OF LIFE

Moreover, so much of music as is adapted to the sound of the voice and to the sense of hearing is granted to us for the sake of harmony; and harmony, which has motions akin to the revolutions of our souls, is not ... given ... with a view to irrational pleasure, which is deemed to be the purpose of it in our day, but is meant to correct any discord which may have arisen in the courses of the soul, and to be our ally in bringing her into harmony and agreement with herself; and rhythm too was given ... for the same reason, on account of the irregular and graceless ways which prevail among mankind generally, and to help us against them...

~Plato, *Timaeus*

Accoording to this quote, the purpose of music is to help us correct any discord in our soul and to give us grace. I have also previously suggested that perhaps the truth can be defined as an idea that *resonates* with many people and therefore an absolute Truth must therefore resonate with *all* people.

In an earlier chapter, I referred to Plato's *The Republic*, in which Socrates describes the just man as one who *harmonises* mind, body and spirit: "[K]eeping all three in tune, like the notes of a scale ... [he] will in the truest sense set his house to rights, attain self-mastery and order, and live on good terms with himself. When he has bound these elements into a disciplined and harmonious whole, and so become fully one instead of many..."

So it seems that grace, truth and justice are to be found in music. It has also been suggested by numerous others before me, that many social and environmental problems today arise because we are not living in *harmony* with nature. So music again.

My question in this chapter is: Why do we use these musical concepts? What does it mean to live in harmony with nature, and what does it mean for an idea to resonate?

In 'The Ecstasy of Yang', I described the idea of yang as the heaven-seeker, the ongoing search for the 'perfect other', or 'the pursuit of heaven'. This search for something different, something better, something more beautiful, continually causes change in our lives and in our societies. We then find this continual change somewhat difficult and so demand some stability, which in turn becomes boring, so we look for more change. This perpetual dance between opposites can be either a struggle or a rhythmical flow. If we always fear change then it will always be a struggle. If we are always looking for change, then we will possibly be creating struggles for others. How can we make it a 'dance between yin and yang'?

I suggested that the yin-yang duality is found throughout our social structures as a reflection of the way our brains are designed. This means that the duality is natural and so also a core element of human nature. We define our life experiences through the highs and lows, indeed the ebb and flow. In winter we wish for summer and in the heat of summer we yearn for cooler weather. We also perpetually search for our opposite, the 'other' that complements us, the other half that completes us. So, why are our brains designed this way and how do these musical concepts relate to our life forces? How do the rhythms of the world around us affect, or perhaps define, life on earth?

Even before Plato, it seems that Moses also believed that the rhythms of nature—this dance between opposites— represented *the* creative force.

> *In the beginning God created the heavens and the earth. Now the earth was formless and empty, darkness was over the surface of the deep, and the Spirit of God was hovering over the waters.*
>
> *And God said, "Let there be light," and there was light. God saw that the light was good, and he separated the light from the darkness. God called the light "day", and the darkness he called "night". And there was evening, and there was morning—the first day.*
>
> ~Genesis 1:1-5

In the beginning, God created the heavens and the earth—that is, the intangible and the tangible, perhaps the imaginary and the real. He then separated the day from the night, the skies from the ground and the land from the seas. The creation of the world required the creation, first, of opposites—light and dark, hot and cold, wet and dry. Not opposites separated by a chasm, but opposites that were two halves of the whole, opposites that flowed or transformed into each other. These are the rhythms of life on earth, the cycles or steady flows from one opposite to the other, from day through to night and back again, from summer through to winter, from high tides to low and so on. Before creating any life, God created a world of rhythms.

The darkness and the light, the imaginary and the real, the fixed and the free, permanence and stability against the inevitability of change. In this chapter, I will aim to illustrate that the rhythmical flow between harmonious opposites creates life. Life is created by the rhythms of the planet, and what we refer to as life is, in fact, the inevitable consequence of a rhythmical planet. In other words, life exists only because our planet has rhythms, and we are bound to the planet through our shared rhythms.

A more thorough understanding of the concepts of rhythm, resonance and harmony, will give important insights into the design of Cities of the future that resonate with nature. To begin, I must explain why I suggest that life exists only because our planet has rhythms. In order to do this, I need to describe what is meant by coupled harmonics, which I can do only through an example.

§

In the summer of 1940, the trend in building ever lighter, more slender and flexible suspension bridges had reached its zenith with the completion of an elegant bridge over Puget Sound at Tacoma Narrows in Washington State, USA. The bridge had a very thin deck and, instead of the traditional open grid trusses along the edges, sleeker, more modern-looking flat-plate girders were used.

As winter approached, the winds in the Puget Sound Convection Zone steadily changed, much as the seasons can cause the winds to change anywhere. On the morning of 7 November 1940, a Thursday, about four months after the bridge had opened, a steady high wind, described as a moderate gale, blew. Much stronger winds had blown the month before and had not affected the bridge.

Some cars drove over the bridge, and the bridge flexed. From the time the bridge was completed, the flex or bounce in the bridge was greater than expected, but studies were being conducted to rectify this, and the bridge remained open to traffic. Some more cars drove over the bridge. There may have been a pause or gap in the traffic and the bridge sprang back towards its static position but overshot that point, as any elastic material will do. Another batch of cars may have arrived in time to exacerbate the original springing action.

Perhaps traffic lights were sending cars in even batches, causing the bridge to spring up and down, but this would have happened on most other mornings since the bridge was built. Perhaps on this day there was little or no traffic from the opposite direction to counter the effects of these traffic movements. Indeed, the rhythm of the car movements is not even mentioned as a possible cause of the following events. Whatever the cause, the rhythmic up and down motion of the bridge began to increase and the deck of the bridge looked like it was flowing like a wave. Soon the wave frequency matched the natural frequency of the structure.

Everything in our natural and built environments has a natural frequency. For long, thin structures, like bridges and the strings of a guitar, this frequency depends on the slenderness, its thickness compared to its length. The material from which it is made and its weight are also important. We tune a guitar in order to find its natural or resonance frequency and we know when it is resonating because it continues to vibrate long after it has been plucked.

That day, the bridge found its rhythm; it resonated. Connected at the ends and also at the two pylons supporting the central span, the deck of the bridge flowed like a wave along its length. Engineers at the scene believed that the wind was causing the vibration and that as the wind speeds changed, the bridge would settle. Then, at about 10.00 am, the bridge began to twist—just a little twist at first. This would not have been a problem if the bridge had the traditional open grid trusses along its sides, because the wind would have flowed through them evenly above and below the deck, steadying the twisting action. Unfortunately, the modern flat-plate girders—solid beams—caught the wind and amplified the twisting. Now the bridge was vibrating along its length as well as across its axis.

If it is possible to ignore the financial consequences, the waste of resources and the loss of the life of a dog trapped in a car, the rhythmic flow of the bridge was beautiful. Have a look at the YouTube video of the Tacoma Narrows Bridge collapse. Two waves, one along the length of the bridge and one causing the bridge to twist on its axis, both continued together for an hour. Surely bolts and cables would start to break and the bridge would slowly tear itself apart during more than a full hour of rhythmic motion. Perhaps the winds would die down and the wave action would stop. Perhaps as some cables broke, the angles would change and the resonating waves would settle.

Suddenly, at 11.10 am, a whole section of the centre span of the Tacoma Narrows Bridge failed. Cables, bolts, girders simultaneously gave way and neatly cut the bridge at centre span. Milliseconds later, another neat cut zapped across the bridge, and a section of deck fell into the water; but why collapse in this fashion? Why such neat cuts, why simultaneous failures of all the elements in one section?

The simple answer is coupled harmonics—two regular but different waves acting on the same object. The peaks and troughs of the long wave moved along the length of the bridge. The wave causing the twisting action alternately peaked on one edge of the deck and then the other at the middle of the centre span. The flexibility of the bridge allowed it to cope with either of the waves acting alone. At 11.10 am, the long wave peaked at the midpoint of the centre span. At that same time the twisting wave peaked its upward motion at one edge, also at the middle of centre span, accelerating the upward motion on this edge. The same twist also peaked in a downward motion at the other deck edge causing the motion on this edge to decelerate. The sudden acceleration on one edge of the bridge and deceleration on the other edge tore the bridge apart. To appreciate the force experienced at this cross-section of the bridge, it is necessary to consider the relative acceleration experienced by the particles at one end compared to the particles on the other edge. The relative acceleration is the ratio of the two accelerations. The upward velocity on one edge suddenly increased, while the same upward velocity on the other edge was cancelled by the downward motion of the twisting wave.

Imagine now if the upward or downward velocity caused by the twisting wave was the same as the velocity caused by the longitudinal wave, then the upward velocity on one edge would double, while the downward velocity on the other edge would be reduced to zero. In calculating the relative acceleration, that is, the ratio between the accelerations on the two edges, the division by zero for the acceleration on the one edge would mean that the relative acceleration on the other edge was effectively infinite.

This is like a shift from one to two on one side while the other edge experienced a shift from one to zero—a shift from one wave complementing another, like a harmony with a melody, to a sudden beat.

Of course, it is unlikely that the waves were exactly equal and indeed the twisting movements appear greater than the longitudinal ones, so the forces may have been close to zero on one side and close to being doubled on the other. Only when the waves are equal will they exactly cancel each other. So infinite power comes only from perfect equality.

Neither resonant wave, acting alone, was able to damage the bridge, so it wasn't resonance alone that brought the bridge down. For the bridge to experience two resonating waves, a number of conditions had to be satisfied simultaneously. The bridge would not have resonated along its length if it had a different length or different thickness or different weight or different combination of these. The bridge would also not have resonated around its twisting axis if it did not have the flat plate edge girders. Had the traffic patterns been different or the wind speed been different or not so consistent, then none of these events would have happened. It was only the combination of all the events acting in a particular pattern at a particular time on an object of a particular design that caused it to experience two resonating waves acting at right angles to each other.

It was the unusual mathematical consequences of two waves, acting perpendicularly to each other, that combined to cause a sudden beat and bring down the bridge.

Now imagine for a moment that the two waves did have the same amplitude. Imagine if, when they synchronised, the waves exactly cancelled each other on one edge of the bridge. The result would be that the acceleration on the other edge, relative to this zero acceleration, would be infinite. This creates a physical problem. A mass moving with infinite acceleration generates an infinite force. An infinite force cannot be contained in a finite location, and so I believe that this is a moment that would be defined as a Big Bang in which a new universe is created.

§

There are various forces in our environment, acting on the objects in that environment. Depending on their shape and the way in which objects are connected to others, the forces can cause them to vibrate. A vibration is a wave action, or a rhythm, with peaks and troughs. All objects have a natural rhythm, a particular rhythm at which the object stores and releases energy very efficiently, this is the resonance frequency. When a force is applied continuously or at the same regular frequency as the natural frequency of the object, then the object will resonate, vibrating according to its natural rhythm. A ribbon-like structure such as the deck of a bridge can have two natural frequencies—one for its long dimension and one for its cross-section for the twisting motion. When two sets of forces create two natural rhythms on a single object, it is possible for the two rhythms to synchronise at some point and compound on each other when the peaks and troughs align. As illustrated in the example of the Tacoma Narrows Bridge, the two synchronised waves can have an explosive effect on the object.

In a world full of rhythms, it is inevitable that there will be an occasional aligning or coupling of those rhythms to create a beat—a sudden and unexpected explosion. Although the alignment of the rhythms and the consequent beat will often have a destructive effect on an object, this is not always the case. If an object is more flexible, less constrained, and able to change, it can survive these impacts. Such objects can be referred to as 'resilient'—that is, able to change and adapt in response to unexpected events. In order to be resilient to any exaggerated and unexpected forces, the object must not resist but rather be designed to transform itself in response to these beats. Imagine a similar ribbon-like structure that resonates in response to two coupling rhythms acting at right-angles to each other. When the powerful beat occurs (and one edge is held still while the other edge experiences an extreme force) the resilient object would allow its entire length to twist around the edge that is held still. In twisting around itself, the ribbon would form a helical shape. The structure of DNA molecules is in exactly this same ribbon-like, double-helix form, like a twisted ladder. DNA molecules contain the genetic instructions for the development and functioning of all known living organisms with the exception of certain viruses, which are based on a single helix form.

As the earth, sun and moon move relative to each other, they create the daily, seasonal, tidal and other cycles that are the rhythms of our planet. There are two categories of objects on the earth, those that have the same natural frequency as the earth's rhythms and so resonate with it and those that do not. Of those that resonate, there are again two categories: those that are resilient to occasional beats and those that are not. Those that are not resilient will break and, by breaking, will form into a new shape or shapes that no longer resonate. The earth's rhythms create a clear distinction between the resilient and resonating 'living' objects and the non-resilient, non-living objects.

Life depends on the ability to be resilient to sudden beats or shocks. A living organism must change. It must be willing and able to transform itself in response to the motions and forces of its environment. Indeed, a living object can be defined as one that is able to change, so to be unwilling to change is to invite one's own destruction.

Change is inevitable and so to be alive is to change.

As each living organism occupies a physical location different from any other, it must necessarily have a different experience of the earth's rhythms, different combinations and extremes of heating and cooling, wetness and dryness and so on. At different latitudes, the length of days and seasons also vary. In the seas and oceans there is an enormous variety of currents, wave actions, pressures at different depths, availability of sunlight, and variations in numerous other conditions. The rhythms will, therefore, marry up or couple in different ways at different times, causing different effects and also resulting in different responses from the affected organism. Those that do not respond to the rhythms and their occasional beats do not survive. Only the most resilient survive to experience further shocks.

The infinite range of possible causes and effects over an extended period of time results in an enormous diversity of responses to the natural rhythms. In addition to the earth's rhythms, each new species provides a new rhythm that can synchronise with others. Every plant and animal species has its own rhythm; some are awake during the day, others at night, some prefer the cold others live in extreme heat, some need very little water, while others need to swim in it; yet all have found a 'natural' rhythm, a pattern of living that works, a way of responding to the earth's cycles. This act of responding to the earth's cycles is the act of living. To simply 'go with the flow', to be swept up by surrounding events, is to be absorbed back into the environment.

To live fully is, then, to act and to respond to the earth's cycles as they present themselves today and, where possible, anticipate any changes in the nature of these cycles.

The most successful species are those that are not only resilient to sudden and extreme beats but which understand their own rhythm and actively seek out other complementary rhythms. Their success is based on connecting with the rhythms of others so as to feel the power of the beat. They seek out the beat because the beat is the moment at which dramatic change is possible, the moment of reproduction or re-creation.

It is a new moment of creation and in every new moment of creation there is renewed hope for a better future.

This seeking out of other rhythms—the search by every harmony for its melody, a marriage of two rhythms—is coupled harmonics. Imagine two bodies in rhythmical motion, connected such that the experience is like two rhythms acting on a single body. Those rhythms assist each other so that the peaks ultimately meet in a single instant. As the two rhythms are very different, even opposite in character, each must encourage the other to grow in amplitude, to reach higher peaks but also to allow the rhythm to fall into a trough before rising again to a higher peak. This rising and falling allows both rhythms sufficient time to harmonise before culminating in an explosion. Each Big Bang is potentially a new moment of creation.

Survival of species doesn't depend only on reproduction but also on the ability to sustain life for a duration, a life-cycle. Some species need to do a certain amount of work in order to assure their survival. For example, insect species such as ants and bees need to work continuously. They form a rigid social structure wherein each individual has a role and the survival of all individuals is dependent on the survival of the queen. By contrast, more developed species such as lions and dolphins will collaborate for just one hour in the day, leaving the remainder of the day for rest, play and pleasure. Mankind alone has the potential to elect how much work is needed to assure survival.

The election to work and the ability to change, to develop and improve over the generations, combine to illustrate one of the most remarkable aspects of the human species. Mankind alone appears to be able to adapt to almost any conditions by choosing to work.

Anthropologists have also demonstrated that our work—that is, our interaction with our tools—has led to physical changes in our body structure. So mankind has developed over an extended period of time by responding to the earth's rhythms, then moving to other locations, adapting to those rhythms by working, then adapting the body to more efficiently use tools and otherwise harmonise with the new environment. This, in turn, allowed movement to other locations, allowing the process to continue. It is an endless process of refinement, of fine-tuning the relationships between the earth's rhythms, our own bodies and our built environment and tools.

So our ability to adapt relies firstly on our ability to understand the earth's rhythms as they express themselves in our particular location, and then on our ability to work in order to harmonise those rhythms with our bodies.

This ability to adapt to any environment, in part by understanding, then adapting the environment to suit our needs, is a unique human trait. Yet if we are capable of altering our environment to support our survival, and if this is, in fact, the defining quality of our species, what does it mean to live in harmony with nature?

To live in harmony with nature cannot simply mean to live in the completely untouched natural environment. Even basic agriculture adapts the environment, so how much can we adapt the environment and still suggest that we are living in harmony with nature?

It could be argued that we are now living more closely to a harmony with nature than ever before because we survive longer and the human population has grown significantly. So perhaps there are many ways of living in harmony with nature. At one extreme, we could try to survive in a completely unaltered environment, that is, align ourselves with nature and live as hunter-gatherers; or, at the other extreme, we could dramatically alter nature to suit us, align nature to our ways. In both cases, we will have harmonised our rhythms with the surrounding environment to assure our survival. Between the two extremes lie an infinite number of possibilities or ways in which our rhythms and those of the natural environment can be harmonised. In order to survive, though, we need to make a decision about how to harmonise with nature, and this will impact on how much work is necessary to achieve this harmony. This decision is our free choice, the expression of our free will.

Irrespective of that free choice, survival requires effort. If we live as hunter-gatherers, that effort will be repetitive and continuous. By making tools that assist us and by altering our environment to support us, we can reduce, although not eliminate, this repetitive and continuous effort. These two types of effort have previously been described and differentiated by Hannah Arendt in *The Human Condition*. She described the repetitive and continuous effort, such as cooking, cleaning and maintenance, as labour and the effort that produces an end product—a tool or a building—as work.

This should assist us when making our free choice about how to live. It is firstly a choice about how much effort, or energy, we need to expend in order to survive. Suppose we make the sensible choice to minimise our total effort. Our next decision is what type of effort, how much labour and how much work? The more work we do, that is, the more labour-saving devices we create, the more our labour could be reduced. Work is not immediately necessary; it is the effort we choose to expend today so as to reduce the labour for tomorrow. It is an investment in the future.

This equation, though, is not as simple as it seems. The more tools and buildings we create, the more labour we create, because these end products require maintenance. Also, if we do not build them well, they will break down, generating more work. If we create more than are necessary or generate by-products, we will create waste, which itself must be managed, generating more labour. If our method of building tools is overly complicated, we will generate labour that has no purpose other than to manage the toolmakers. As the process becomes more complicated still, we can create further labour, whose purpose is nothing more than to try to understand the complexity of the system we have created.

So is there an optimum—a perfect balance between work and labour that will minimise our total effort? In fact there is. Our choices and priorities determine the rhythms of our life, and our growing life expectancy is sufficient proof that we are living in harmony with nature. How much work is required to assure that survival, though, relates to resonance. Our resonance frequency is the particular rhythm of life in which our environment stores and releases energy efficiently and in doing so dramatically reduces the amount of work we need to do. Although our current systems have been successful in increasing life expectancy, they also generate more work for individuals than ever before.

Tools and technology were once regarded as labour-saving devices. To find our resonance frequency (and it is different in every location) requires that we view everything we build, our cities, our homes, our tools and technology as the means by which we can reduce our work and our labour. Do our homes save us from work or create work? Are our tools designed to last, or are they designed to quickly become obsolete so as to increase the private interests of the tool builder? Most things we construct generate more work and more maintenance. The things we own are a burden because they do not resonate with us, they do not store and release energy efficiently, they do not work for us, they create work for us.

So resonance relates to the ability of an object to efficiently store and release energy—that is, to do work so that the work and labour we need to do is reduced. If our homes and our cities stored and released energy efficiently, they would capture the heat of the day and release it at night. That is, they would be oriented towards the sun to capture its warmth, and they would have the thermal mass necessary to store that heat and release it at night. They would also capture and store the rain and the light when it falls and release energy and water as it is needed. They would be designed in alignment with the rainfall patterns in that location and capture water so that there is sufficient continuous supply for the population of the area.

With regard to tools, rather than building 'consumables',—products that are used once and then discarded—we would perhaps build 'durables' that, with a little maintenance would last for an extended period of time. Ideally, we would build 'sustainables'—that is, end products that can be sustained indefinitely.

The more we align our homes with the natural rhythms at their location, the more of our work the home and tools can do for us. Our homes would also capture the productive capacity of other plants and animals to produce food and deal with waste. The more we allow and facilitate nature to work for us, the less work we will need to do; and the more our environment will resonate with us.

14

FENCING THE ECONOMY

O People! just as you regard this month, this day, this city as Sacred, so regard the life and property of every Muslim as a sacred trust. Return the goods entrusted to you to their rightful owners. Hurt no one so that no one may hurt you. Remember that you will indeed meet your Lord, and that he will indeed reckon your deeds.

Allah has forbidden you to take usury [interest], therefore all interest obligations shall henceforth be waived. Your capital is yours to keep. You will neither inflict nor suffer any inequity. Allah has Judged that there shall be no interest and that all the interest due to Abbas ibn 'Abd al-Muttalib [the Prophet's uncle] be waived...

~The Last Sermon of the Prophet Muhammad

It appears to me that the central theme in the battle of ideas throughout history has been the question of how to fence the economy—how to limit the pursuit of wealth so as to find the time and space for the things we value more. There is no more relevant question to the organisation of a City than to ask 'How do we free ourselves from work so as to create the opportunity for creativity, spirituality, relaxation and enjoyment; how do we provide the time and space for love and for community and for doing great deeds in service of others?

Moses sought freedom from slavery and suggested that one day in seven should be a day of rest. Homer said that in order to distinguish yourself and to do great deeds, you must *not* spend your limited days tied to your fate, your obligations and responsibilities but, instead, you must pursue your destiny.

Socrates said, "For I do nothing but go about persuading you all, old and young alike, not to take thought for your persons and your properties, but first and chiefly to care about the greatest improvement of the soul. I tell you that virtue is not given by money but that from virtue comes money and every other good of man, public as well as private."

Jesus said, "Come to me all you who are weary and burdened and I will give you rest" (Matthew 11:28). I believe that this 'rest' will come by adhering to his words: "Do not lay up for yourselves treasures on earth … For where your treasure is, there your heart will be also. … No one can serve two masters…" (Matthew 6:19-24). That is, no one can pursue wealth and at the same time share their wealth, or have freedom from work, or pursue the good of others in the community. So rather than competing to maximise treasures on earth (by working harder or enslaving others to work for you), rest from work, do the things that you love, pursue your destiny and do good deeds such as giving to others so that they also are not burdened by work.

Siddhārtha Gautama, known as the Buddha, encouraged us to follow the Middle Way, the way of moderation and so away from the extremes of self-indulgence and also away from extreme asceticism.

In *The Analects*, Confucius taught that: "To be wealthy and honoured in an unjust society is a disgrace."

Solon of Athens cancelled all debts. He did this to address a situation in which revolution was imminent because the revolutionaries could see no escape from the bondage of perpetual indebtedness. Despite continual repayments and austerity, the growing interest ensured that the total would never be repaid. In many such cases today, the original capital has been paid many times over.

In Judaism, this approach was enshrined as a law and is known as the 'biblical jubilee' of Deuteronomy 15:1; "At the end of every seven years you must cancel debts."

The need to *regularly* cancel debts arises because the root of the problem was not addressed by this cancellation. It did not change behaviour or perceptions of wealth. It therefore did not address the inequality caused by material wealth. Individuals simply return to the same practices, incorporating the consequences of the jubilee into their financial plans. Muhammad's approach learns from the biblical jubilee and tackles this underlying problem. He says: "Your capital is yours to keep." There is no harm in capital, in money, in trade, or in economics as a means of ensuring that everyone's needs are satisfied. The harm arises through the charging of interest. Harm stems from the investment practices of our day that encourage us to invest our capital and make our money work for us. Money cannot work for us. The interest we charge ensures that others are forced to work for us.

Should we take advantage of others simply because fate was generous to us? We inherit good fortune and then invent systems that aim to enhance our good fortune at the expense of the less fortunate. Effectively, our systems are designed to increase inequality, to create and maintain and reinforce a hierarchy. We need those who are less fortunate to remain there so they can work for us. We seem to believe that this is how the world should be, or that there is nothing we can do to change it, or that dispensing a little charity from our excess is sufficient.

When Muhammad said, "Hurt no one so that no one may hurt you ... You will neither inflict nor suffer any inequity", he reiterated the Golden Rule described by Buddha, Confucius and Jesus. They all sought equality. Jesus and Mahatma Gandhi did not humble themselves to highlight their own greatness but to elevate the least fortunate to a position of equality, to illustrate what equality looks like.

Muhammad's approach required that capital obligations be repaid, while interest obligations were waived and interest on future loans was forbidden. I acknowledge that if you have lent money, it should be repaid; we would regard this as a matter of basic morality. What, though, is the moral standing of a money-lender who lends money at high interest in full knowledge that the borrower will never be able to repay the capital? Read David Graeber's *Debt: The First 5,000 Years* for a fuller exploration of the moral confusion surrounding debt throughout history.

If money is to be used, its purpose is to facilitate the flow of goods and services throughout the society. To save money for a future purpose is reasonable, but to hoard money so as to make others work for you through their interest 'obligations' is not. When individuals hoard money in this way for their own private benefit, they reduce the supply of money in the economy, which is the root cause of economic cycles, economic recessions and eventually, collapse.

Some will suggest that this is all very interesting in theory, but there is no chance that banks will agree to charge zero interest or that governments will implement and enforce policies to require this. Of course they won't, as the position of centralised authorities is founded on this inequality. This is why imagining the world as a network of local village-scale communities is an imperative. At the village scale, it is not necessary to gain approval from such authorities. In a community of this size, there will be some who are financially wealthy and some who are indebted. It would benefit both groups to cancel debts owed to external financial institutions. The wealthy most often are saving for their retirement to ensure they are cared for when they are no longer able to work. By relieving the debt burden of others in the community, they are doing a good deed that will one day by returned in kind when they are in need. They are building social capital, bonds within their community and creating an environment of equality. Most precisely, they are relieving others of work, gifting them the free time during which care may be offered.

It is therefore clear in my mind that certain essential principles are involved in fencing the economy. The first is that a community must be of a small scale so that all citizens know one another. This ensures that when one does a good deed, it is recognised and known within the community, ensuring that such deeds are repaid, not in kind but in accordance with needs. Trust and honour are developed through doing good deeds for others rather than by accumulating wealth and authority for yourself. In 'Transparency, Democracy, Liberty' I described how, prior to the invention of coins in about 600 BCE, the principal means by which many communities evaluated credit-worthiness was on the basis of this community trust.

Using the internet, individuals can now also build a less complete but still very useful kind of trust and reputation in a global network of villages through the sharing economy. Comments left on collaborative consumption websites form a trail of your activity and character, enabling others to gain a small insight into your past and judge whether you are trustworthy. New websites, such as TrustCloud.com, are being developed so that individuals can take control of the trust trail they have generated across numerous collaborative websites.

Our current system of creating a public, or work, identity that is different from our private identity is inauthentic and so prohibits the development of trust.

The second essential principle, then, relates to this relationship between public and private, a key theme in this book. Certain things are not meaningful when completely privatised. As described above, money serves a public function, facilitating the flow of goods and services through the society.

204 FENCING THE ECONOMY

When it is privatised, hoarded by a few individuals, this directly affects the flow within the economy.

The same applies to the use of knowledge, information and ideas, which serve a similar public function. The purpose of these is to facilitate communication in the society, which aids its positive development. Their availability to all in the society benefits all, while when these are kept secret for the benefit of a few, inequality is created and the entire society suffers.

To achieve equality in the society requires an appreciation of the relationship between public and private. When referring to money and knowledge, these should be fully public. With regard to identity, though, the public and private must be identical, there is only one identity. When building a physical City, both public and private spaces are essential. The relationship between public and private varies depending on the subject, neither is good or bad, they are just different, like yin and yang in Chinese philosophy.

In this physical City, some of the public spaces could be used to house visitors and so could become private spaces during these visits. In 'The Ecstasy of Yang,' I described how a community should actively seek to identify gaps in skills and fill these by inviting new citizens. In that chapter, I described the manner in which communities would produce food and housing in excess of their needs so that they could exchange these for the skills of visitors. This exchange would further reduce the need for the money-based economy. These visitors could be chosen on the basis of the trust they had built in the sharing economy.

The first principle for fencing the economy is therefore to create the optimal conditions for trust to develop; and the second is to optimise the various relationships between private and public. The third principle for fencing the economy is to maximise efficiency. In 'The Rhythm of Life', I described how a built environment that resonates with nature works for us and therefore limits the amount of work we need to do. Limiting work reduces the scale of the economy and the total energy demand. When the environment is designed to provide most of the water and energy for a community and also deals with its waste, then the economy does not need to build the major infrastructure works that transport these across the landscape. When that environment also provides food and housing, then trade in these is also unnecessary. The economy needs to provide only those goods and services that are not available within the community. Enhancing the natural environment therefore further reduces the activity within the fences of the economy. We should continually be on the lookout for ways of reducing the total amount of required work.

Other infrastructure that would become redundant is the major transportation infrastructure required for the daily commute, which would be eliminated if we constructed our cities on the basis of a single authentic identity, located in one place, rather than our current private and professional identities. It is highly inefficient to waste time every day moving to and from work and home at the same time as everyone else just to create the illusion of a different self. This is not to preclude the separation of work spaces from private sanctuaries within walking distance of each other in a village.

The reason for limiting the scale of the overall economy is the same as that used by economists keen to achieve economic growth. That reason is, again, efficiency. Economists often use the term loosely so as to maximise profits—the difference between outputs and inputs. For example, they argue that by reducing input costs or by increasing the price of the output, producers will maximise their profit margin. The focus tends to be on this profit margin rather than on either the inputs or the outputs.

Instead of focusing on costs, the emphasis should be on total energy usage. From this perspective, the scientific definition of efficiency can be used, and this relates to optimising the *ratio* of output energy to input energy or, given a particular output requirement, finding the least energy input needed to achieve this. The most efficient economic system is one that resonates—that stores and releases energy efficiently. It is a system in which the processes are arranged so that there is minimal energy usage.

How can these processes achieve minimal energy usage? All economic processes consist of people and buildings in a place. Energy is wasted if the people travel long distances to their workplace. Energy is wasted if other inputs need to travel to that place. Energy is wasted if sun falls and it is not captured, either by solar panels or by plants that provide food for the people. Energy is wasted if the buildings are not built using passive design to naturally heat and cool. Energy is wasted if rain falls and is not used for irrigation or for some other need either of the people, their economic process or the environment.

Striving towards efficiency implies that our economic systems should be seeking to minimise rather than maximise work. They would support natural systems and minimise wastage.

§

All of the above principles are connected to the issue of scale. For example, in the first principle, I stated that communities must be small in scale to develop trust. Yet how small is small? In the third principle, I suggested that if we know the output we could minimise the inputs to achieve maximum efficiency. So again we need to know the scale of the City so as to know the output demand.

In 'Renaissance of the Polis' I also argued that the scale of the city is important because, as the City grows, economic efficiency theoretically grows, but democracy and participation is reduced because the voice of each citizen is diluted. This suggests that there may be an optimal size for a City.

Let us address this issue in a number of steps, determining firstly whether an optimal and therefore fixed size is appropriate and then determining what that size may be.

The fundamental problem in economics is to manage fluctuating supply and demand, and this is why we have a market in which price is negotiated. Is it possible to imagine that supply and demand are not always variable? If the scale of the City is fixed, that is, it has a known population, it is possible to determine the level of demand, at least for basic necessities.

With a city of fixed population, it is possible to establish how many private sanctuaries are necessary, how many shared spaces of different sizes, and how many kitchens, laundries and other facilities are needed. The amount of food, energy, water, clothing and other materials could also be fixed. Given this broadly fixed demand, it is then possible to determine supply requirements, including what and how much can be provided internally and what needs to be sourced externally. With fixed supply and demand, there is no need to negotiate price. There is no need for a market for the basic necessities of life. Indeed, by planning to have an over-supply of food and accommodation, it becomes possible to host guests, as described earlier, who could, in exchange for this excess food and free accommodation, provide some goods or services not otherwise available within the community.

So the first step is to adopt the principle that it is desirable to fix the population, the next step is to ask *how* should the population be fixed.

As previously described, the design of our global City as a network of local Cities allows each of these to be fixed and then, if the population grows, the community itself is responsible for the work necessary to build a sister community. Each would be responsible for managing its own basic needs and its own population.

I have also described how ancient communities in Greece recognised the limits of their natural environment and, rather than sprawling their City, they built trading partner sister-states. This approach was, of course, not unique to Greece and was the approach of all traditional agricultural and pastoral communities. Each community was essentially responsible for managing its own population.

So the two initial steps were, firstly, to agree on the need to fix the scale of each community and, secondly, to do this by establishing a global network of communities; the next step is to talk about actual sizes. I preface this next section by stating that each locality is different. Each has different rainfall, different access to fresh water, different solar and climatic conditions, different geography and so on. As a result, the answer will be different for each such locality and community. The building of communities within existing urban environments should also not be precluded although these will likely require trading partner communities in rural areas to provide some foods.

Nevertheless, I believe that there are some broad ideas that could be considered for the scaling of cities.

Let's begin by imagining the proposed village-scale community as a cluster of smaller hamlets which, in turn, are a cluster of private sanctuaries. Scaling upwards, Cities and larger communities would be formed through the networking of these villages. The scales would then be: private sanctuary (individual suite for one person), household, hamlet, village and then City.

Imagine, then, at the household scale, a collection of six sanctuaries for six individuals. These individuals may be members of the same family, or three couples, or six unconnected individuals or any combination of these. Rather than assuming that all households will house a family (in Sydney, Australia, 22 per cent of households are occupied by a single person, while another 30 per cent are occupied by couples without children), perhaps it is most efficient to design households to flexibly accommodate six individuals.

Six households could then be clustered to form a hamlet housing up to thirty-six individuals, which is the size of a clan. Six hamlets could then be clustered to form a village of up to

216 citizens. If, or as, the village population approaches this number the aim would be to build a sister-village rather than expand or sprawl the village.

Despite the fact that this will be described as social engineering, the reality is that humans have gathered at the household, clan and village scales for much of human history. The orderly scaling mimics the manner in which natural systems are similar at different scales—this is the fractal organisation of nature as patterns that repeat themselves.

The household with its six sanctuaries is designed to accommodate all individuals, irrespective of their stage in life or marital status, that is, it is inclusive rather than designed exclusively for families. Costs and maintenance responsibilities are always shared by up to six, rather than one or two individuals and, in this sense, the burden of work and the demands of economics are shared more widely and therefore significantly reduced for all.

Grouping households into a cooperative clan ensures that, at that scale, most foods will be able to be provided, while by further expanding the scale and clustering six hamlets to form a village, many specialist trades, clothing manufacture, household maintenance, medical care and so on could all be provided internally.

This grouping and scaling not only manages supply and demand but also ensures that citizens always see that they are a part of something bigger. Rather than each individual limiting his or her concern to the household, there are feedback benefits to stepping outside the household and ensuring that the hamlet and the village are functioning smoothly so that a range of goods and skills will then be freely available. Also, in this arrangement there is a place for everyone, irrespective of their circumstances or stage in life. For example, there will be a meaningful role for the elderly, young parents will not be unreasonably burdened by the demands of child care, children will have a broader range of influences, and being single is less likely to translate into being lonely.

To finish off on the question of village scale, there is also the evidence of anthropologist Robin Dunbar, who argues that when a group exceeds approximately 150 individuals it ceases to function as a single cohesive unit and begins to splinter into smaller groups. This suggests that the scale of the village ought to be less than the proposed 216.

Dunbar argues that the neo-cortex, the part of the brain that deals with complex thought and reasoning, is also responsible for managing human relationships, because its size increased as our means of gathering food became more complex. Through studies that compared the size of the neo-cortex of other primates and their group sizes he calculated that the size for human groups should be approximately 150. Dunbar also referenced numerous studies of various human groups and found a high level of consistency, with many group sizes in the order 150-200 individuals. For example, Neolithic villages are generally understood to have had a population of approximately this size, as do many modern tribal communities.

So if human communities should be of this size, then I would imagine that a village could have a *capacity* for 216 individuals but housing a core community of 150. The spare capacity could be occupied by young, non-contributing children as well as visitors who will bring skills that are not available within the community but are necessary at a particular time, as previously discussed.

I believe that imagining the global City as a network of interconnected villages, each of which manages its own environment, is an important aspect of fencing the economy. If each community could strive towards self-sufficiency, providing most of its own food, water, energy and other private necessities, then it would be less dependent on broader complex systems and infrastructure, making each more resilient.

If each village community also produces some more complex good or provides a more specialised service to other villages then it would become a ready replacement for the corporation. It would provide the goods and services required by the broader society and would also provide the forum for creativity, exciting new discoveries and new ways of doing things. So, although each village should strive towards self-sufficiency, each should also acknowledge that this is like striving towards infinity. It is unachievable; and it may also be undesirable to be completely self-sufficient. Any individual, household or community that is completely self-sufficient has no need of others outside of it. It is the things that we are unable to do ourselves, as well as those gifts that we offer freely to others that build the connections between us.

The aim for each household, clan or village should be to strive towards self-sufficiency so as to satisfy private needs as efficiently as possible. This allows more time to be spent on a broader, more challenging purpose, a public purpose, a purpose that requires creativity and innovation and satisfies the needs of others outside your community.

In this way, each individual, and communities at all scales, are ensuring that everyone has their needs satisfied and everyone is also provided with the opportunity to contribute to something greater. The inward focus creates a sense of community while the outward focus provides connections to the rest of the world. The two become complementary rather than conflicting.

The City should therefore be designed to provide public spaces of numerous types at every scale to allow individuals to contribute to a public purpose at the scale at which they are most comfortable.

The collaborative spaces at the household, hamlet and at the village scales ensure that the purpose of the collaboration determines the number of people involved and the scale of the spaces.

§

As a final note, I'd like to pose the question: "How will this change occur, and who will likely drive the change?"

I believe that many of these changes will be driven by the collective actions of individuals who are concerned about our shared social and environmental problems. Such individuals are already acting to convert their towns into 'Transition Towns', some are building eco-villages, cooperative housing schemes and other intentional communities. All are designing local solutions to global problems.

The builders of intentional communities, though, are only creating one part of the solution. The other part of the solution is being built by the creators of the sharing economy and other forms of online collaboration. This alternative economy will replace the current profit-driven economy and provide the network links between the various local communities.

It has also become evident that corporations are likely to also play a significant role in the transition by transforming themselves.

In recent years, especially in the IT industry, innovative corporations such as Google (see YouTube: 'life at Google') are providing a range of facilities including free food for breakfast, lunch and dinner, free gymnasium, sports and entertainment facilities, personal trainers and doctors, places to sleep, and shared electric cars. These 'benefits' satisfy the basic needs of the employees, so that they can focus their energy on the company's purpose. Employees then do not become distracted by their private needs because the company ensures that these are all satisfied efficiently and, where possible, on-site. The distinction between the private and the public is being realigned in accordance with the original basis for the division. The private relates to the satisfaction of basic needs for survival, while the public relates to your contribution to something bigger, something that serves others outside your 'private' community. These do not need to be in different spaces.

The Google campus is not considered a perfect system, but it does illustrate a different way of understanding the difference between public and private. Perhaps the next step for Google is to provide the housing of its community but the step that follows that will be the real hurdle, transforming the hierarchical, privately owned corporation into a company of equals.

Ultimately, it is important to recognise that our entitlement to have our basic needs satisfied should not be dependent on our 'productivity' or our earning capacity any more than on our fate. Our first obligation to each other is to ensure that everyone feels that their basic needs are satisfied. This is fundamentally what it means to treat each other as equals. Our work can then be the free gift of each individual to others, each according to their capacity to give.

The Google campus is interesting from a town planning perspective because it is a community of people who share a common vision located in the same place. It is consistent with the model of a village that strives towards self-sufficiency but also offers an outward-looking purpose that requires creativity and innovation and satisfies the needs of others outside that community.

Through the example of the Google campus, it is possible to see the development from social networking, which is just talk, to public networking, which is social networking that consists of a community working with a common purpose. When that community is located in a particular place, it creates a 'City' that provides the private needs of the citizens as efficiently as possible so as to create as much freedom for them to do the one thing they all love doing.

§

Are we willing to re-imagine our Cities? Are we willing to act and bring that imagined ideal City to life? Do we want a world in which our role is simply perpetual work for the supposed benefit of future generations, or is it possible to create a world in which the objectives are to build trust, encourage transparency and authenticity, offer freedom and pursue happiness?

Can we evolve beyond the childhood phase of human development in which everything is mine, mine, mine? Can we imagine a world in which we have learnt to share and in which we favour access over ownership?

Can we create a world in which we think of each other as equals?

Can we rethink the City? What we think, we become!

EPILOGUE:

PROPOSED TRANSITION CHARTER

1. Transition, that is, continual and steady change, is our process for creating a Better World.

2. Our Better World will be a global network of intentional local communities.

3. The network will be forged through but bound only by the free sharing of all human knowledge.

4. Each community shall regard all other communities as their equals and is responsible for sharing knowledge to achieve and maintain that equality.

5. Each community shall strive towards self-sufficiency with respect to food, water, energy and material resources, with this to be achieved by resonating with the natural environment in the locality of the city.

6. Each community acknowledges that the right to use any part of the Earth is accompanied by a responsibility to maintain or enhance the health of the Earth so it may also be used by all future generations of all life species.

7. Each community shall maintain itself at a scale whereby all its members can meaningfully participate as equals in the development of agreements that bind the community together.

8. Each community shall allow and encourage the continual review of its agreements so that those social contracts are suitable to the present participants.

9. Each community shall allow and encourage the free movement of individuals between communities.

10. Each community acknowledges that all individuals are unique and therefore different but, nevertheless, all are regarded as equals.

11. Each community shall encourage all individuals in their pursuit of self-knowledge, which is the pursuit of happiness.

12. Through the pursuit of self-knowledge, achieved by enabling freedom from work, accepting change and encouraging personal growth, we can each discover how we can contribute freely to the creation of a Better World.

BIBLIOGRAPHY

Amunugama, E. (1994). *The History of Ancient Aryan Tribes in Sri Lanka*. Colombo, Sri Lanka: J.R. Jayewardene Cultural Centre Publication

Anthony, C. K. (1981). *The Philosophy of the I Ching*. Anthony Publishing Company

Arendt, H. (1958). *The Human Condition* (2nd (1998) ed.). The University of Chicago

Aristotle. (2002). *The Athenian Constitution* (2nd ed.). (P. Rhodes, Trans.) Penguin Classics

Aristotle. (1992). *The Politics* (3rd ed.). (T. Sinclaire, Trans.) Penguin Classics

Auel, J. (1980) *The Clan of the Cave Bear* (Coronet 2002 ed.). London: Hodder and Stoughton

Auel, J. (1982) *The Valley of the Horses* (Coronet 2002 ed.). London: Hodder and Stoughton

Auel, J. (1985) *The Mammoth Hunters* (Coronet 2002 ed.). London: Hodder and Stoughton

Bettencourt, L. M. (2013, June 21). The Origins of Scaling in Cities. *Science*, 1438-1441

Bible - New International Version (NIV)

Botsman, R. a. (2010, September 14). *Huffington Post*. Retrieved October 24, 2013 from Huff Post Books: http://www.huffingtonpost.com/rachel-botsman/goodbye-hyperconsumption-_b_716107.htm

Botsman, R. (2010, May). *The Case for Collaborative Consumtion*. Retrieved October 24, 2013 from TED - Ideas worth spreading: http://www.ted.com/talks/rachel_ botsman_the_case_for_collaborative_consumption.htm

Braudel, F. (2002). *The Mediterranean in the Ancient World* (3rd ed.). Penguin Books

Castoriades, C. (1997). The Greek Polis and the Creation of Democracy (1983). In C. Castoriades, & C. D. A. (Ed.), *The Castoriades Reader* (pp. 267-289). Blackwell Publishers

Chander A., et al. (2004). The Romance of the Public Domain. *California Law Review* , 1331-1373

Clogg, R. (1992). *A Concise History of Greece.* Cambridge University Press

Daly, H. (2007). *Ecological Economics and Sustainable Development, Selected Essays of Herman Daly.* Great Britain: MPG Books Ltd

Daly, H. (1992). *Steady State Economics.* London: Earthscan Publications

Dunbar, R. (1993). Co-Evolution of Neocortex size, Group size and Language in Humans. *Behavioural and Brain Sciences, 16* (4), 681-735

Ehrenberg, V. (1973). *From Solon to Socrates - Greek History and Civilization During the 6th and 5th Centuries BC* (2nd ed.). Methuen & Co

Freeman, C. (2005). *The Closing of the Western Mind, The Rise of Faith and the Fall of Reason.* Vintage Books

Ghonim, W. (2012). *Revolution 2.0.* London: Fourth Estate (Harper Collins)

Gladwell, M. (2000). *The Tipping Point - How little things can make a big difference.* Great Britain: Little, Brown

Graeber, D. (2011). *Debt: the first 5,000 years.* New York: Melville House Publishing

Hamilton, C. (2003). *Growth Fetish.* Allen & Unwin

Hamilton, P. J. (1922). The Civil and the Common Law. *Harvard Law Review* , 36 (2), 180-192

Hammond, N. (1986). *A History of Greece to 322BC* (3rd ed.). Oxford University Press

Hardin, G. (1968). The Tragedy of the Commons. *Science* , 162, 1243-1248

Kirkpatrick, D. (2010). *The Facebook Effect, The Inside Story of the Company that is Connecting the World.* Simon & Schuster

Klooger, J. (2009). *Castoriades: Psyche, Society, Autonomy.* Leiden-Boston: Brill Publishing

Krotoski, A. (2010, May-June). *The Virtual Revolution.* (M. Milton, Producer, & BBC) Retrieved October 28, 2013 from www.bbc.co.uk: http://www.bbc.co.uk/ virtualrevolution/about.shtm§

Lang Ho, C. (2013). *Spontaneous Interventions.* From http://www.spontaneousinterventions.org: http://www. spontaneousinterventions.org/interventions

Meadows, D. M. (1972). *The Limits to Growth: a Report for the Club of Rome's Project on the Predicament of Mankind.* New York: Universe Books

Meadows, D. R. (2004). *A Synopsis - Limits to Growth - The 30-Year Update.* Hartland: Chelsea Green

Pepalasis, A. A. (1959). The Legal System and Economic Development of Greece. *The Journal of Economic History* , 19 (2), 173-198

Plato. (2003). *The Republic* (2nd ed.). (D. Lee, Trans.) Penguin Classics

Plato. (2004). *Timaeus*. (B. Jowett, Trans.) Adelaide: eBooks@Adelaide, Creative Commons Licence

Quinn, D. (1992). *Ishmael*. New York: Banter

Rajanayagam, S. (1994). *Thus We Became - From Beginning to Civilisation, and Dravidian History to World War II.* Colombo, Sri Lanka: Lake House Investments Book Publishers

Ratcliff, E. (2011, March). Taming the Wild. *National Geographic Magazine* , 219 (3)

Ryan, A. (2012). *On Politics, A History of Political Thought from Herodotus to the Present*. London: Allen Lane, an imprint of Penguin Books

Saul, J. R. (1993). *Voltaire's Bastards - The Dictatorship of Reason in the West* (2nd ed.). Penguin Group

Suzuki, D. a. (1997). *The Sacred Balance, Rediscovering our Place in Nature*. Allen & Unwin

Todd, M. a. (2013, May 28). Retrieved May 28, 2013 from The Conversation: http://theconversation.com/open-publishing-is-happening-the-only-question-is-how-13100

Tolle, E. (2005). *A New Earth, Create a better life*

Turner, G. (2007). *A Comparison of the Limits to Growth with Thirty Years of Reality*. CSIRO. Canberra: CSIRO

Turner, M. (2009, October 29). *Sweet, Unmingled, a potion divine - Greek Wine from Antiquity to Modern Times.* (E. Bollen, Performer) Nicholson Museum, The University of Sydney

Ware, T. K. (1993). *The Orthodox Church* (3rd ed.). Penguin Books

Weintraub, J. (1997). The Theory and Politics of the Private/Public Distinction. In J. a. Weintraub, & W. a. Kumar (Ed.), *Public and Private in Thought and Practice - Perspectives on a Grand Dichotomy.* University of Chicago Press

www.ingramcontent.com/pod-product-compliance
Lightning Source LLC
Chambersburg PA
CBHW020857270326
41928CB00006B/751